Christmas activities

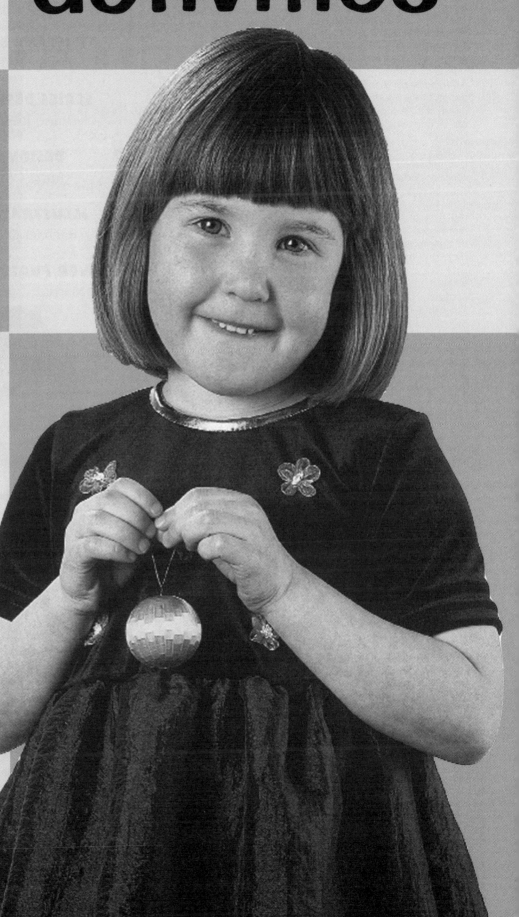

CREDITS

British Library Cataloguing-in-Publication Data
A catalogue record for this book is available from the British Library.

ISBN 0 439 01898 6

The right of Lisa Bessinger to be identified as the author of this work has been asserted by her in accordance with the Copyright, Designs and Patents Act 1988.

All rights reserved. This book is sold subject to the condition that it shall not, by way of trade or otherwise, be lent, hired out or otherwise circulated without the publisher's prior consent in any form of binding or cover other than that in which it is published and without a similar condition, including this condition, being imposed upon the subsequent purchaser.

No part of this publication may be reproduced, stored in a retrieval system, or transmitted, in any form or by any means, electronic, mechanical, photocopying, recording or otherwise, without the prior permission of the publisher. This book remains copyright, although permission is granted to copy pages 57 to 80 for classroom distribution and use only in the school or by the teacher who has purchased the book and in accordance with the CLA licensing agreement. Photocopying permission is given only for purchasers and not for borrowers of books from any lending service.

ACKNOWLEDGEMENTS
The publishers gratefully acknowledge permission to reproduce the following copyright material:

Jillian Harker for 'Eric's Christmas toys' © 2001, Jillian Harker, previously unpublished; Trevor Harvey for 'The angel who is different' © 2001, Trevor Harvey, previously unpublished; Brenda Williams for 'Welcome baby Jesus' © 2001, Brenda Williams, previously unpublished; Peter Morrell for 'Ring-a-ding, ding!' © 2001, Peter Morrell, previously unpublished.

Every effort has been made to trace copyright holders and the publishers apologize for any inadvertent omissions.

AUTHOR
Lisa Bessinger

EDITOR
Jane Bishop

ASSISTANT EDITOR
Lesley Sudlow

SERIES DESIGNER
Lynne Joesbury

DESIGNER
Anna Oliwa

ILLUSTRATIONS
Rachael O'Neill

COVER PHOTOGRAPH
Martyn Chillmaid

Text © 2001 Lisa Bessinger
© 2001 Scholastic Ltd
Designed using Adobe Pagemaker
Published by Scholastic Ltd, Villiers House,
Clarendon Avenue, Leamington Spa, Warwickshire CV32 5PR
Printed by Bell & Bain Ltd, Glasgow
Visit our website at www.scholastic.co.uk

34567890   4567890

CONTENTS

5 INTRODUCTION

CHAPTER 1
Personal, social and emotional development

9 CRACKER SURPRISE!
10 OUR CHRISTMAS TREE
11 NATIVITY QUILT
12 PIÑATA
13 CHURCH OUTING
14 DRESS THE SHEPHERDS
15 CHRISTMAS WALL PLAQUE
16 MY HANDS WREATH

CHAPTER 2
Communication, language and literacy

17 I WOULD LIKE FOR CHRISTMAS...
18 WELCOME BABY JESUS
19 MYSTERY CHRISTMAS PRESENTS
20 CHRISTMAS PUDDING TRUFFLES
21 BETHLEHEM BELLS
22 CHRISTMAS CAROLLERS
23 CHRISTMAS BINGO
24 MY FAVOURITE STORY

CHAPTER 3
Mathematical development

25 FIND THE MISSING SHAPE
26 WHICH TREE IS THE TALLEST?
27 MY CHRISTMAS STOCKING
28 THE WAY TO BETHLEHEM
29 SORT THE DECORATIONS!
30 COUNTDOWN TO CHRISTMAS
31 PIN THE STAR ON THE TREE
32 PRESENTS GALORE

CHAPTER 4
Knowledge and understanding of the world

33 STAINED-GLASS WINDOW
34 IT'S A WRAP
35 EUROPEAN SPICY BISCUITS
36 STARS IN THE BETHLEHEM SKY
37 LET'S PARTY
38 NATIVITY SCENE
39 CHRISTMAS LONG AGO
40 MY CHRISTMAS WISH

CONTENTS

CHAPTER 5
Physical development

41	CHRISTINGLE
42	LITTLE BABY JESUS
43	GOLD AND SILVER GARLAND
44	FOLLOW THAT STAR!
45	FATHER CHRISTMAS' WORKSHOP
46	CHRISTMAS WREATH TARGET
47	IN AND OUT THE SNOWMEN!
48	ON OUR WAY TO BETHLEHEM

CHAPTER 6
Creative development

49	RUDOLPH REINDEER PUPPET
50	CHRISTMAS WONDERLAND
51	ALL KINDS OF ANGELS
52	CHRISTMAS DRAWING BOXES
53	ZIGZAG NATIVITY BOOK
54	CHRISTMAS BAND
55	CRACKER CHRISTMAS CARDS
56	A WISE MAN

PHOTOCOPIABLES

57	ERIC'S CHRISTMAS TOYS
58	THE ANGEL WHO IS DIFFERENT
59	WELCOME BABY JESUS
60	RING-A-DING, DING!
61	PULL A CRACKER
62	CHRISTMAS TREE
63	PIÑATA
64	SHEPHERDS GAME
65	LETTER TO SANTA
66	CHRISTMAS PUDDING TRUFFLES
67	CHRISTMAS TREES
68	CHRISTMAS STOCKING
69	GOING TO BETHLEHEM (1)
70	GOING TO BETHLEHEM (2)
71	HOW MANY?
72	STAINED-GLASS ANGEL
73	STARS
74	PLAY DOUGH RECIPE
75	COCONUT-ICE BALLS
76	ACTION!
77	SHEEP
78	FIND THE WAY
79	IN A STABLE
80	CANDY CLAY RECIPE

Introduction

This book forms part of a series of books providing a wide range of exciting, stimulating and fun practical activities for early years children. The ideas cover all six Areas of Learning encompassed in the Early Learning Goals (QCA) for pre-school children but are equally appropriate for the documents on pre-school education published for Scotland, Wales and Northern Ireland. This book provides 48 separate activity ideas in an easy-to-use format and 24 photocopiable sheets all aimed at four-year-olds, with support and extension for children aged between three and five years of age.

The festival of Christmas

As one of the most important and exciting religious festivals of the year, Christmas is a time of great joy for Christians all over the world as they celebrate the birth of Jesus Christ two thousand years ago. Even for non-Christians, Christmas is a major celebration. It is a time when family and friends get together, sharing meals, giving and receiving presents and cards, and going to church. Shops and homes are decorated and children look forward to a visit from Father Christmas!

Often the true meaning of Christmas is lost through commercialism and the 'hustle and bustle' that surrounds Christmas with advertising and shop window dressings for Christmas beginning months in advance. It is therefore vital to draw the children's attention to the true meaning of Christmas and to explain why it is such an important religious festival in the Christian calendar.

The wide range of activities in this book provide opportunities to understand and learn the true religious meaning of Christmas such as

INTRODUCTION

'Church outing' on page 13, providing children with a respect and awareness of Christian beliefs. Other activities reinforce the nativity story through various mediums, for example, 'Welcome baby Jesus' on page 18, provides a nativity play and in 'Nativity quilt' on page 11, the children make a group quilt using pencil crayons and coloured card. The more traditional aspects of Christmas are also covered in 'Countdown to Christmas' on page 30 and 'Rudolph reindeer puppet' on page 49. Other activities show the children how people in different countries, such as Mexico, celebrate Christmas, as in 'Piñata' on page 12. Children are also encouraged to share their personal experiences with the other children in the group such as in 'My Christmas wish' on page 40.

Aim to balance out the materialistic aspects of Christmas by making the children aware of other people and their feelings, and how it is important to think of others over the festive season, for example, in 'Cracker surprise' on page 9 with the making of a gift for a family member.

How to use this book

The six chapters in this book each cover a different Area of Learning identified by the QCA in its document *Curriculum guidance for the foundation stage* and each contain eight separate activities. The areas covered are Personal, social and emotional development, Communication, language and literacy, Mathematical development, Knowledge and understanding of the world, Physical development and Creative development.

The activities all follow the same format, starting with a clearly stated 'Learning objective'. An ideal 'Group size' is given together with an estimate of how long each activity will take. These are both flexible and need to take into account the children and staff available at your setting. 'What you need' states all items required and where appropriate 'Preparation' details any necessary planning required. The main activity idea is described in 'What to do' and is aimed at an 'average' four-year-old. The two sections 'Support' and 'Extension' give practical suggestions for adapting or extending the main activity to suit younger or less able children, and older or more able children respectively.

INTRODUCTION

The 'Home links' section offers ideas to help establish a sound link between the children's homes and your setting. This might include asking parents and carers to continue developing skills at home, providing items for use at your setting or coming in themselves to share in the fun! 'Multicultural links' are also suggested when relevant to help the children to gain or maintain an awareness of other countries and cultures, festivals and traditions.

Some of the activities require a minimum amount of adult preparation such as 'Father Christmas' workshop' on page 45, whereas others require more such as 'Mystery Christmas presents' on page 19.

Encourage the children to help with any preparation whenever possible and, in some cases, reduce preparation by using resources from more than one activity, for example, 'Stars in the Bethlehem sky' on page 36 and 'Gold and silver garland' on page 43. Some of the activities require the whole group's participation such as 'Pin the star on the tree' on page 31, whereas others such as 'My hands wreath' on page 16 concentrates on small groups of children.

Using the photocopiable sheets

Each chapter has four supporting photocopiable sheets on pages 57 to 80 that are used in different ways. Some can be used by the children to complete at your setting such as 'Christmas tree' on page 62 and others can be taken home to complete under the supervision of their parents or carers such as 'Find the way' on page 78. Other sheets contain recipes such as 'Candy clay recipe' on page 80 and others give templates such as 'Christmas stocking' on page 68. New resources such as a story, a poem, a play and a song are also included.

Resources

Pre-school children learn best through hand-on activities, talking, active participation, repetition, asking questions and solving problems, all of which require concrete experiences. Many of the activities in this book make use of a wide variety of different resources including books, paints, crayons, paper, sand and so on which are available in most pre-school

INTRODUCTION

settings. Other activities require specific materials such as Christmas decorations that you will need to collect or purchase in advance of carrying out the activity. If possible, involve parents and carers in collecting any items required.

Links with home
The link between the children's homes and your group is an important one, which cannot be overemphasized. Whatever the children learn with you can be reinforced at home so that there is continuity in their education. At the end of each activity you will find a small 'Home links' section containing a practical suggestion of how parents and carers can be actively involved in their child's learning. The word 'carers' has been used alongside 'parents' to address other members in a child's world who may look after them in place of parents.

You can actively encourage parents, carers or grandparents to participate in activities at your setting such as in 'Christmas long ago' on page 39, when you can invite family members in to share memories of Christmas when they were young. They can also be involved in the preparation of food for the 'Let's party' activity on page 37.

Multicultural links
Many of the activities provide a multicultural idea to provide the children with a greater understanding of how different cultures and nationalities celebrate Christmas throughout the world. In some cases, it forms the main activity such as in 'Piñata' on page 12. The main aim is to encourage children to respect, be tolerant of, and sensitive to the individual difference and cultural backgrounds of others. Encourage the children and parents and carers of different nationalities to share their own traditions with the other children by talking to them about how they celebrate Christmas.

It is very important to remember that for those children in your setting who are not Christians, and whose parents do not want them to participate in activities relating to Christmas, there are always sufficient additional activities for them to complete so that they do not feel excluded. Their individual religious beliefs should always be respected and sensitivity shown towards them.

CHAPTER 1

Personal, social and emotional development

This chapter provides a range of activities focusing on personal, social and emotional development. Children are encouraged to work together and respect the needs and beliefs of others. The activities will inspire the children to take turns and share, learn about different cultures and become aware of Christianity.

GROUP SIZE
Two or three children.

TIMING
15 minutes.

CRACKER SURPRISE!

Learning objective
To develop an awareness of other people's feelings.

What you need
Felt or fabric which will not fray; glue; spreaders; kitchen-roll tubes; aprons; lengths of coloured ribbon; craft knife; selection of pot pourri; plastic bowls; pinking shears; scissors; sequins; foil squares.

Preparation
Cut the felt or fabric into 20cm squares and cut the kitchen-roll tubes in half. Use the craft knife to make several holes in each one to let the scent out. Place the pot pourri and other materials into plastic bowls.

What to do
Talk to the children about Christmas as a time of giving to other people as well as receiving. Explain that what matters is not the size or price of a present but the love and thought which goes into choosing or making it. Tell the children that they are going to make a special cracker and ask them who they would like to give their cracker to and why.

Invite the children to cover a section of kitchen-roll tube with glue, to choose a piece of fabric and stick this to the tube, ensuring an equal amount of fabric, approximately 4cm, is left at both ends. Ask each child to hold their cracker while you pull the fabric together on the lower end, tying it tightly closed with a piece of ribbon. Next, ask each child to smell the pot pourri and to fill their cracker with a selection through the open end. While the children are working, talk about the different smells and ask them what they remind them of.

When each cracker is full, tie the open end closed, in the same way as before. Ask the children to decorate their crackers using the sequins and foil squares. Show them how to use the pinking shears on the overlapping pieces of fabric to finish the crackers. Explain that the cracker can be placed in a drawer among clothes to make them smell nice.

Support
Help younger children when using tools such as the pinking shears.

Extension
Invite older children to think of other containers for the pot pourri.

HOME LINKS
Give parents and carers a copy of the photocopiable sheet on page 61 and ask them to help their children complete it at home.

Personal, social and emotional development

GROUP SIZE
Whole group.

TIMING
20 minutes to make tree; 15 minutes to make and hang decorations.

OUR CHRISTMAS TREE

What you need
Plaster of Paris; plastic bucket; wooden spoon; small stones; small branch with plenty of twigs; aprons; paint; paintbrushes; glue; spreaders; silver glitter; plant pot; wax paper; small bells; coloured foil; pencils; scissors; bodkin; glittery wool; length of tinsel; egg-box bases; the photocopiable sheet on page 62.

Preparation
Mix some green paint with glue and silver glitter. Cut the coloured foil into strips. Cut the cups off the egg-box bases. Line the plant pot with a piece of wax paper.

HOME LINKS
Suggest that parents and carers point out different types of Christmas trees when they are out and about with their children, in garden centres or at the local shops.

What to do
Make up a batch of plaster of Paris in a plastic bucket following the instructions on the packet. When the mixture is the consistency of cream, stir in some small stones. Ask one child to hold the plant pot while another holds the branch steady in the pot. Carefully pour the plaster of Paris mix around the branch and leave to set. When dry, lift the 'tree' carefully from the pot and peel off the wax paper. Show the children how to paint the 'tree' green and paint the base using coloured paint. (NB Do not dispose of any excess plaster of Paris mix down the sink as it will harden and may block the drain.)

Divide the children into smaller groups to make the decorations. To create icicles, wind a foil strip tightly around a pencil, remove the pencil and thread a piece of wool through the top of each icicle before hanging. Scrunch pieces of foil into balls and join them together with wool and a bodkin to make foil garlands to drape around the tree.

Make egg-box bells by covering egg-box cups with pieces of foil. Tie a bell to a piece of wool and thread it through a hole in the top of each egg-box cup before tying to the tree. Finish by tying a piece of tinsel around the base of the tree.

Finally, give each child a copy of the photocopiable sheet to complete.

Support
Limit the choice of decorations to just two types for younger children.

Extension
Invite older children to wrap some 'presents' to place under the tree.

Personal, social and emotional development

GROUP SIZE
Small groups.

TIMING
15 minutes for pictures; 20 minutes for quilt.

NATIVITY QUILT

Learning objective
To contribute to a group project, to feel a sense of pride in personal achievement.

What you need
A roll of heavy wallpaper; A4 sheets of coloured cardboard; coloured corrugated cardboard; pencil crayons; silver and gold stars; container; aprons; glue; spreaders; sticky tape; scissors; nativity story such as *The First Christmas* (Dolphin); card; shoebox; marker pen.

Preparation
Join two equal lengths of wallpaper down the back with sticky tape. Cut out seven cards, approximately 21cm x 5cm each, from the coloured cardboard and write one element of the nativity story on each card, for example:
- Angel tells Mary that she is going to have a baby.
- Mary and Joseph go to Bethlehem.
- Innkeeper says there is no room at the inn and they have to stay in a stable.
- Baby Jesus is born in the stable and laid in a manger.
- Shepherds are tending their sheep when angels appear and tell them to go to see baby Jesus.
- Shepherds go to Bethlehem to worship baby Jesus.
- Three Wise Men follow the star to see baby Jesus.

Place the cards in the shoebox, the stars in a container and other materials on the table.

What to do
Read the story of the birth of baby Jesus. Explain that the children are going to make a nativity quilt telling the story. Invite each child to pick a card from the shoebox and encourage them to read what is written on the card. Now, ask each child to draw a picture relating to what is written on the card. Continue until all the cards have been chosen and there are seven pictures.

Ask the children to sort the caption cards and pictures into their correct story sequence before placing them on the wallpaper. Stick the pictures down with the correct captions, leaving a space between each picture and card. Arrange corrugated strips of card between the pictures and captions to form a border and glue down. Decorate the quilt with silver and gold stars. Once dry, hang the quilt on the display board and 'read' the story to the children. Stress that each child's picture has made the story quilt complete.

Support
Help younger children with the laying out of their pictures and the sticking.

Extension
Older children can help to write the captions for the pictures and take turns to 'read' the nativity story.

HOME LINKS
Ask parents and carers to draw their children's attention to the correct sequence of a story and how it always has a beginning, middle and end.

Personal, social and emotional development

GROUP SIZE
Whole group.

TIMING
20 minutes.

PIÑATA

Learning objective
To learn about a different culture.

What you need
Books about Christmas in Mexico such as *Merry Christmas – Children at Christmas time Around the World* by Satomi Ichikawa (Heinemann); blindfold; strips of newspaper; large round balloon; piece of string; coloured paint; paintbrushes; tinsel and streamers; wallpaper glue; two bowls; sticky tape; the photocopiable sheet on page 63; length of ribbon; stick; wrapped sweets; chocolate coins; small paper bags; scissors.

Preparation
To make the Piñata, inflate a large balloon, tie a piece of string over the knotted end and cover with two layers of strips of newspaper dipped in wallpaper glue, leaving a space open at the bottom. Allow the first layer to dry before applying the second. When dry, burst the balloon and pull out using the attached string. Paint and allow to dry before turning the Piñata over so that the hole is now at the top. Attach strips of tinsel and coloured streamers to the base with sticky tape. Make two holes next to the hole in the top and thread a length of ribbon through both for hanging. Place the wrapped sweets and chocolate coins inside and fill the hole with a length of tinsel.

What to do
Talk about different countries and how they celebrate Christmas in their own ways. Show the children pictures of children celebrating Christmas in Mexico and in particular pictures of Piñata.

Hang the Piñata from the ceiling by the attached piece of ribbon ensuring that is not too high. Explain how, in Mexico, children are blindfolded and given turns to hit the Piñata so that it will break. Invite each child to take a turn at doing this with the option not to wear the blindfold. Make sure that the other children stand well clear of the child swinging the stick. When the Piñata breaks, it will shower its contents on the ground. Ask the children to collect the treats and place them in a bowl. Give each child a small paper bag and divide the sweets between them. Finally, give each child a copy of the photocopiable sheet to complete.

Support
Help younger children to swing the stick.

Extension
Ask older children to suggest different shapes for the Piñata, for example a fish or owl shape.

HOME LINKS
Send a letter to parents and carers outlining what you have been doing and explaining how to make a Piñata by filling a paper bag with a few sweets and hanging it up.

Personal, social and emotional development

GROUP SIZE
Whole group.

TIMING
30 minutes for outing; ten minutes for book.

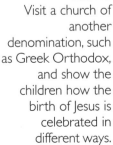

HOME LINKS
Encourage parents and carers to take their children to a service at their local church over the Christmas period.

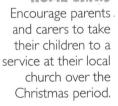

MULTICULTURAL LINKS
Visit a church of another denomination, such as Greek Orthodox, and show the children how the birth of Jesus is celebrated in different ways.

CHURCH OUTING

Learning objective
To create a respect and awareness of Christianity.

What you need
Length of white cotton fabric (quantity will depend on size of group); A4 sheets of cardboard; scissors; coloured permanent marker pens; ribbon; aprons; stapler; needle; gold wool; pinking shears.

Preparation
Arrange a visit to your local church and ask parents and carers to accompany you. Cut the white cotton fabric into pieces slightly bigger than A4. Pull each piece taut as you staple each to a sheet of A4 cardboard.

What to do
Visit the local church and ask the minister to give a short talk about the birth of Jesus and how Christians celebrate His birth. Encourage the children to ask questions.

Back at your setting, talk about what you saw and heard, encouraging all the children to share their ideas and observations. Next, invite each child to put on an apron and to use marker pens to draw something relating to the church visit on the cardboard covered by the white fabric. Close supervision is required to ensure that the ink from the pens does not get on clothes, skin or other children.

When all the drawings are complete, remove the fabric from the cardboard and cut around the edges of each picture using pinking shears.

Make a book by placing the fabric pictures between two pieces of card and sewing down the left-hand side using the needle and gold wool. Write each child's name in the top left-hand corner of their drawing and number each picture in sequential order. On the cover of the book, write the name of your setting and the date that you visited the church. Invite the children to take turns to look through the book before placing it where parents and carers can look at it.

Support
Keep all discussions short and within the comprehension of younger children.

Extension
Let older children write their own names on their pictures.

EARLY YEARS ACTIVITY CHEST Christmas activities

Personal, social and emotional development

GROUP SIZE
Four children.

TIMING
15 minutes.

HOME LINKS
Invite parents and carers to take the game home to play with their children. Encourage them to play other board games using dice.

DRESS THE SHEPHERDS

Learning objective
To take turns within a group and to select resources independently.

What you need
Four pieces of A4 white card; four pieces of A4 coloured card; sticky-backed plastic; scissors; the photocopiable sheet on page 64; felt-tipped pens; coloured spot stickers; dice.

Preparation
Copy the photocopiable sheet and cut off the figure. Copy the figure onto four A4 pieces of white card and the clothing/accessory pieces onto four pieces of coloured card. Mark each piece of clothing/accessory with a coloured spot sticker ensuring that there are six loose clothing/accessory pieces for each figure. Cover the pieces of cardboard with sticky-backed plastic, cutting out only the clothing/accessory pieces and leaving the figure boards whole.

What to do
Give each child a baseboard with the figure of a shepherd on it and place the loose clothing/accessory pieces face upward in the centre of the table. Talk to the children about shepherds at the time of baby Jesus' birth and how their clothing was very different from that worn by people in our country. Explain that in some hot countries such as Africa, some shepherds still wear clothing like the shepherds did in Jesus' time.

To play the game, each player rolls the dice and counts out loud the number of dots shown. The first player to roll one dot starts by picking up a card piece with one dot on it from the pieces in the centre of the table. Place this piece over the correct area on the shepherd's outline. Point out that the tunic will go over the shepherd's underwear and so on.

If the child rolls the dice and he already has that piece then he misses a turn and the next child takes a turn. The first child to complete their shepherd is the winner with the game continuing until all the shepherds are complete. The two sheep can be placed alongside the shepherd.

At the end of the activity, explain to the children that when all the pieces are placed on the shepherd baseboard they make up a whole image.

Support
Help younger children to find the correct pieces to place in their correct position.

Extension
Ask older children to help with the making of the game.

EARLY YEARS ACTIVITY CHEST Christmas activities

Personal, social and emotional development

GROUP SIZE
Small groups.

TIMING
15 minutes.

CHRISTMAS WALL PLAQUE

Learning objectives
To select and use a widening range of resources independently; to experiment with different materials.

What you need
Plastic vegetable or cake trays (in a variety of shapes); plaster of Paris; wax paper; red powder paint; plastic straws; bodkin; scissors; selection of old Christmas decorations; wooden spoon; plastic jug; glitter; aprons; permanent black marker pen; lengths of different-coloured ribbon; containers for decorations.

Preparation
Make a batch of plaster of Paris in the plastic jug following the instructions on the packet. When the mixture is the consistency of cream, add the red powder paint and mix well. Cut the straws in half and the wax paper into sizes slightly bigger than each tray.

What to do
Invite each child to wear an apron and choose one of the plastic containers as a mould to form the base for a plaque. Line each container with a piece of wax paper before pouring approximately 3cm of plaster of Paris into each one. Push a piece of straw through the plaster of Paris approximately 2cm from the top of the plaque and leave in place. Ask each child to choose any of the Christmas decorations and to press these into the plaster of Paris in interesting patterns. Ensure that they push the bigger decorations, such as balls, down firmly.

Talk to the children about how it feels when they press each decoration into the plaster of Paris. Encourage them to tell you which Christmas decorations are their favourite and why. (NB Do not dispose of any excess plaster of Paris mix down the sink as it will harden and may block the drain.)

When the children have finished, invite them to sprinkle glitter over their plaque while it is still wet. Allow the plaster of Paris to dry for approximately one hour before lifting each plaque from its mould. Peel off the wax paper and cut the piece of straw, which is sticking out, flush against the plaque. Push the piece of plaster of Paris that is inside the straw out using a bodkin. Ask each child to choose a piece of ribbon before threading it through the straw in the plaque using the bodkin. Tie a knot in the two ends of ribbon so that the plaque can be hung. On the back of each plaque, write the child's name and the date using a permanent black marking pen.

HOME LINKS
Ask parents and carers to let you have any old Christmas decorations that they can spare.

Support
Let younger children choose from just two or three types of decorations.

Extension
Encourage older children to sort the decorations into different categories, balls, tinsel and so on or by colour or size.

Personal, social and emotional development

GROUP SIZE
Small groups.

TIMING
15 minutes.

MY HANDS WREATH

Learning objective
To maintain attention in making an individual creation.

What you need
Thick card approximately 15cm x 15cm in a variety of shades of green; round cake tin with a hole in the middle; plastic bottle-top lids; red paint; paintbrushes; uncooked green pasta twirls and pasta bow shapes; scissors; glue; spreaders; pencils; aprons; containers.

Preparation
Trace around the inner and outer circles of the cake tin. Cut around the outer circle and fold in half, making sure that the second circle's line is facing upwards. Cut along this line and open up the circle to leave a circle with a hole in the middle. Ask the children to help paint the bottle-top lids red. Place the pasta twirls, red bottle-top lids and pasta bow shapes into separate containers. Put these and all the other materials on the table.

What to do
Talk to the children about evergreen Christmas wreaths and how they form a very important part of traditional Christmas celebrations, symbolizing hope and love. Explain that they are going to make a wreath in the traditional Christmas colours of green and red. Ask each child to choose a number of squares of green card and to trace carefully round their hands. Talk about hand shape and size and how everyone's hand is different from another person's as we are all individuals. Ensure each child makes enough handprints to go around their circle base. Cut out the hand outlines and ask each child to lay their handprints around the cardboard circle, trying out different patterns and positions before sticking them down. Show the children how to cover the handprints with glue and stick on the green pasta twirls and the red bottle-top lids, and finally place a pasta bow shape somewhere on the wreath.

Support
Help younger children to trace around their hands and cut out the outlines.

Extension
Let older children trace around the cake tin and cut out the wreath circle base themselves.

HOME LINKS
Invite parents and carers to draw their children's attention to the different types of wreaths on people's front doors when they are out and about.

MULTICULTURAL LINKS
Make a traditional Mexican poinsettia ('flower of the holy night') hands wreath using red paper instead of green paper for the leaves.

Tell the children the story of the poinsettia about a little Mexican peasant girl who wanted to give baby Jesus a present but, being so poor, had nothing to give. While she sat outside a church crying, an angel appeared and pointed to a patch of weeds, which she picked. Walking into the church with her present, the weeds started changing colour until they were the stunning red of the poinsettia.

CHAPTER 2

Communication, language and literacy

In this chapter you will find a range of activities for children to develop their communication, language and literacy skills. These include taking part in role-play, understanding how English is written and read, learning the words of a new carol, as well as developing listening skills.

GROUP SIZE
Small groups.

TIMING
15 minutes.

HOME LINKS
Ask parents and carers to save used envelopes. Encourage them to take the opportunity to show their children how we read and write from left to right and from top to bottom, whenever possible.

MULTICULTURAL LINKS
Tell the children about a German custom in which children write letters to the Christ child asking for presents and sprinkling sugar on the envelopes. They hope that the sugar will sparkle and catch his eye as he passes their window with his basket of presents.

I WOULD LIKE FOR CHRISTMAS...

Learning objective
To know that print carries meaning and in English is read from left to right and top to bottom.

What you need
Medium-sized cardboard box; red paint; paintbrushes; black marker pen; cotton wool; pencil crayons; glue; spreaders; sticky-backed address labels; the photocopiable sheet on page 65; used envelopes with stamps; sticky tape; craft knife.

Preparation
Tape together both ends of the box and invite the children to help you to paint it red. When dry, use the craft knife to cut a slot in the front for the letters to fit through. Cover the top of the box with cotton wool for snow and write 'Letters for Father Christmas' on the front with the marker pen. Make a copy of the photocopiable sheet for each child.

What to do
Talk to the children about what they would like for Christmas and encourage them to give reasons for their choices. Ask them if they have been good and what they consider good behaviour to be.

Give each child a copy of the photocopiable sheet. Start at the top of the letter and point out what they need to fill in. Stress a left to right movement and explain that we always read and write from left to right and from top to bottom. When they have finished, ask them to read their letter to the group. Let them choose an old envelope, stick one of the address labels over the old address and write 'Father Christmas, Lapland' on the envelope, copying the words from the top left-hand corner of their letter. Finally, ask the children to post their letters in the post-box.

Support
Scribe the words for younger children and encourage them to illustrate their letters.

Extension
Encourage older children to write their own letters, providing any unknown words for them.

Communication, language and literacy

GROUP SIZE
Whole group.

TIMING
20 minutes.

WELCOME BABY JESUS

Learning objective
To take an active part in and role-play specific characters.

What you need
The photocopiable sheet on page 59; length of coloured cardboard; paper; hat; toy fluffy animals; selection of everyday clothing; doll's cot; A4 piece of paper; pen.

Preparation
Write the names of the characters, excluding Mary and Joseph, on separate pieces of paper, fold in half and place in the hat. Make a copy of the play on the photocopiable sheet.

What to do
Read the play to the children explaining that it is a modern day version of the nativity story. Explain that everyone will have a part, dress up and sing carols (see 'Christmas carollers' on page 22). Place the names of the older girls in a hat and pick one to play Mary; repeat with the older boys to choose Joseph. Ask each of the other children to take a piece of paper from the hat to allocate the further roles. Encourage the children to think about what they will need to wear for their parts in the play. Stimulate discussion by asking them to think about what they have at home which might be suitable. Write down all their ideas and suggest other items, for example, the angels could wear party dresses; shepherds could wear sun-hats, boots, old shirts and trousers; Joseph could carry a suitcase; Mary could wear a long dress; the Wise Men could wear bright and colourful clothing with crowns (card decorated with sequins and cotton wool) and carry modern-day gifts; a doll's cot could be used as the crib.

HOME LINKS
Send home a letter to parents and carers asking for costumes for the play. Invite them to attend the final production.

The play starts with just the narrator (adult) who is then joined by Mary and Joseph. Slowly the numbers increase until all the children form a tableau. The children will need to practise the play a few times in order to remember the sequence of actions. Encourage some children to say a few words and let all the children join in singing the carols.

Support
Encourage younger children to take part, pairing them with older children if necessary.

Extension
Older children could make invitations inviting parents and carers to see the play.

Communication, language and literacy

GROUP SIZE
Small groups.

TIMING
15 minutes.

MYSTERY CHRISTMAS PRESENTS

Learning objective
To develop critical thinking and use language to describe something.

What you need
A3 sheet of paper; marker pen; scissors; ruler; Christmas wrapping paper; assortment of everyday items; boxes and containers in different shapes; sticky tape; card; scissors; ribbon; paper and stick-on labels.

Preparation
Wrap the everyday items disguising their identity, for example, by placing a pencil in a margarine tub. Stick a label, numbered 1 to 5, on each parcel. Cut the card into pieces approximately 10cm x 10cm and write a few clues on each, for example, for a piece of soap write 'Something we use to wash with'. Attach the card to the parcel with a piece of ribbon. Draw up a grid on the A3 sheet of paper with the children's names in the first column and five further numbered columns.

What to do
Talk to the children about Christmas in Holland and how presents are given on 6 December which is known as Saint Nicholas Eve. Explain that presents are wrapped to disguise their contents and that clues are written on pieces of card. Show them the presents that you have wrapped and tell them that they are going to pretend to be Dutch children and try to guess, using the clues, what is inside each parcel. Encourage them to use all their senses.

Pick up each parcel in turn and ask individual children to describe what they can feel, what they think is inside the present and why. Read the clues on the label to help them guess. Encourage them to move it slowly, from side to side, and to listen carefully to what is inside. Tell them to smell the present as this may help if it is something scented, such as a bar of soap. When each child has had a chance to guess each parcel, write their ideas on the chart next to their names.

Finish the activity by gathering the children together and unwrap the parcels in turn. As each present is opened, look at the chart and see who, if anyone, was correct in his or her assumption. Talk about why they made their guesses.

Support
Limit the number of presents to just three for younger children.

Extension
Encourage older children to find something in the room, wrap it up and ask other children to guess what is inside.

HOME LINKS
Explain to parents and carers what you have been doing and encourage them to let their children guess what is inside their presents before they open them.

EARLY YEARS ACTIVITY CHEST Christmas activities

Communication, language and literacy

GROUP SIZE
Four children.

TIMING
15 to 20 minutes.

CHRISTMAS PUDDING TRUFFLES

Learning objective
To follow a pictorial recipe.

What you need
For each child: apron; small plastic bowl; child-size rolling-pin; pastry board; teaspoon; blunt knife; chocolate strands; two teaspoons of drinking chocolate powder; three digestive biscuits; two teaspoons of condensed milk; icing sugar; water; angelica; red cherries; the photocopiable sheet on page 66; sticky-backed plastic; Christmas pudding; A4 card; tea towel.

Preparation
Cut the angelica into small pieces to form 'holly' leaves, and the cherries to form 'berries'. Prepare a bowl of white glacé icing and cover with a damp tea towel until ready for use. Copy the photocopiable sheet onto four pieces of card and cover with sticky-backed plastic. (NB Check for any food allergies or dietary requirements.)

What to do
Help each child to put on an apron, then ask them to wash their hands and to each sit with a pastry board in front on them. Show the children a real Christmas pudding and explain that it is a traditional pudding eaten after the Christmas meal on Christmas Day. Give each child a copy of the pictorial recipe. Point to the top of the page and show them where the instructions start and how to follow it by working across and down the page. Explain how to start by crushing two digestive biscuits and putting the mixture in a bowl and then move on to the next step.

Show the children how to measure out the correct ingredients using the teaspoons and explain that they need to follow the recipe carefully.

As the children work, talk about where they are up to in the recipe and what comes next. If the mixture is too thick, add more condensed milk, if too thin, add more icing sugar. When each child's mixture is the right thickness, ask them to roll it into a ball shape and then roll it in the chocolate stands until coated. Dribble a small amount of white icing on top of each 'pudding' before sticking on the 'holly' and 'berries'.

Finally, drop a small amount of icing on top of the third biscuit and attach each Christmas pudding truffle.

Support
Help younger children to 'read' the pictorial recipe by talking through what they can see in the pictures.

Extension
Invite older children to make their own pictorial recipe.

HOME LINKS
Send home a copy of the recipe for the children to share with their parents and carers.

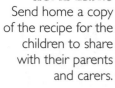

Communication, language and literacy

GROUP SIZE
Small groups.

TIMING
15 minutes.

BETHLEHEM BELLS

Learning objective
To develop listening skills.

What you need
Small bells; thick length of ribbon; needle and thread.

Preparation
Make a set of 'Bethlehem bells' by sewing a number of small bells, evenly spaced, onto a length of thick ribbon. Sew the two loose ends of the ribbon together.

What to do
Gather the children together in a circle on the floor and show them the bells. Explain how what we can hear does not depend on what we can see; it is a separate skill. Demonstrate by asking the children to close their eyes while you walk to a corner of the room and ring the bells. Ask them to point to where the sound is coming from and then let them open their eyes to see if they were correct.

Return to your original position and tell the children about a little angel who the Angel Gabriel asked to keep the Bethlehem bells safe (ring the set of bells in your hand) until baby Jesus was born. The angel waited and waited and soon became so tired that he fell asleep with the bells next to him.

Choose one child to be the little angel who must sit on the floor in the middle of the circle with his eyes closed and the bells beside him on the floor. The other children ask 'Are you sleeping little angel?' to which he replies 'Yes'. Point to another child who must creep up to the angel, pick up the bells and ring them loudly before returning to his seat with them. Ask all the children to place their hands behind their backs. Ring the bells again and say 'Wake up little angel, someone has taken the Bethlehem bells'. The angel wakes up and must try to identify who has taken the bells by pointing to that child. If they are not sure, let the child holding the bells shake them again. The child who took the bells now takes a turn at being the angel.

Let the children continue playing until they have all taken a turn at being the angel.

HOME LINKS
Encourage parents and carers to play games that require listening skills such as 'Sound Lotto' with their children.

Support
Work in very small groups with younger children as it will take time for them to be able to recognize where the sound of the bells is coming from and who is holding them.

Extension
Invite older children to think of additional listening games that they could play together.

Communication, language and literacy

GROUP SIZE
Whole group.

TIMING
15 minutes.

HOME LINKS
Invite parents and carers to share other songs and carols with their children.

MULTICULTURAL LINKS
Ask parents and carers of different nationalities to come to your setting to sing one of their traditional carols in their native tongue, or they could make a tape recording to be played to the children!

CHRISTMAS CAROLLERS

Learning objective
To learn the words of a new carol.

What you need
The photocopiable sheet on page 60; musical instruments (see 'Christmas band' on page 54); six A5 sheets of card; marker pen; medium-sized box; flannel board, pieces of Velcro.

Preparation
Write out the three different sections of the song 'Ring-a-ding, ding!' onto separate pieces of card, writing either A or B on each one. Attach a piece of Velcro to each card. Place each child's musical instrument in the box ready for use.

What to do
Sing a number of well-known songs and carols with the children, some of which can be used with the nativity play (see 'Welcome Baby Jesus' on page 18) such as 'Away in a Manger' and 'Silent Night'.

Tell the children that you are going to teach them a new carol. Sing the carol to them, placing each card on the flannel board as you sing. When you finish, ask if anyone noticed anything about the song. Explain that the carol has three sections, with the first section being repeated. Show them this on the cards, which is known as ABA. Make sure that the children know the carol before giving out the musical instruments.

Divide the children into two groups, 'A' and 'B'. Explain that when you point to card 'A' on the flannel board, all the children in that group must play their instruments. When you point to card 'B', the children in the 'A' group must stop playing and the 'B' group children start. Stress that they must look carefully at which card you are pointing to in addition to singing the carol at the same time. Let the children choose a carol in which they can all play their instruments together such as 'We Three Kings'.

Support
Concentrate on just the carol during one session with younger children and introduce the musical accompaniment at another time once they are familiar with the carol.

Extension
Encourage older children to make up a song to a well-known tune with an ABA pattern.

Communication, language and literacy

GROUP SIZE
Six children.

TIMING
15 minutes.

CHRISTMAS BINGO

Learning objective
To help develop visual perception.

What you need
Card; scissors; Christmas wrapping paper (make sure you have doubles of each Christmas picture); glue; spreaders; sticky-backed plastic; shoebox and lid; tinsel; marker pen; ruler; sticky tape.

Preparation
Make bingo cards by cutting twelve pieces of cardboard into squares approximately 20cm x 20cm and ruling lines to divide each piece into three vertical columns and two horizontal. Cut out two identical pictures from the sheets of Christmas wrapping paper and stick one to two of the baseboards. Continue until all the baseboards have six pictures on each with each baseboard having a double. Cover both sets with sticky-backed plastic before cutting one of each of the sets into six separate cards. Cover the shoebox with wrapping paper and a strip of tinsel and place the cards inside.

What to do
Give each child a baseboard and explain how to play the game. Ask them to study the pictures on their boards very carefully and say that for each picture on their board, there is a matching card in the box. Tell them that you will hold up one card at a time and they must study it carefully, before looking at the pictures on their board to see if they have the matching card. Each time you hold up a picture ask the children to say what it is and to look to see if they have the picture on their board. If no one recognizes that they have the card on their board, put it back in the box and continue. If anyone does recognize it, they must place the picture card over the corresponding picture on their board. The child who has all the cards on their board is the winner and must call out 'Bingo'.

Continue playing until all the boards are full before checking them to see if they are all correctly matched. Let the children change boards and repeat as long as the children are interested.

HOME LINKS
Ask parents and carers to play games which require visual perception such as *Snap* or *Bingo* with their children.

Support
Limit the number of pictures on each baseboard to four for younger children.

Extension
Use pictures that are quite similar to each other for older children to ensure that they look very carefully at the details.

Communication, language and literacy

GROUP SIZE
Whole group.

TIMING
15 minutes.

MY FAVOURITE STORY

Learning objectives
To share favourite books; to develop listening skills.

What you need
Clean lolly sticks; each child's Christmas book brought from home; coloured card approximately 10cm x 7cm; felt-tipped pens; sticky tape; spreaders; two empty coffee tins; Christmas wrapping paper.

Preparation
Cover both coffee tins with Christmas wrapping paper. Invite each child to bring in their favourite Christmas book and ask them to write their name and the title of their book on a piece of coloured card. Arrange all the books neatly on a Christmas display table. Attach each name card firmly to the top of a lolly stick with sticky tape before placing them in one of the coffee tins.

What to do
Talk to the children about the variety of books on display and how everyone likes different books as we are all individuals and enjoy different things. Show all the books to the children, setting an example by handling each one with great care and respect. Demonstrate how you must always turn the pages of books very carefully so that they do not tear and explain that when you have finished reading, you should put them back in their correct places.

During story time, and over a number of sessions, randomly pick one stick from the coffee tin and ask the children to tell you whose name is written on it. Ask the named child to find their book from among those on the table. Encourage the child to tell the others in the group why this is their favourite book. Many children will not want to do this so encourage them to say something if possible. Share the chosen book with the children and ask them questions about the story.

Finally, place the name stick that has just been used in the second tin so that it will not be chosen again.

Support
Help younger children to write the names and book titles on the pieces of card.

Extension
Encourage older children to show their chosen book to the other children. If they are very familiar with it they may be able to tell the story themselves.

HOME LINKS
Encourage parents and carers to visit the local library with their children to borrow a variety of fiction and non-fiction books about Christmas.

MULTICULTURAL LINKS
Invite parents and carers of different nationalities to visit your setting and ask them to read or tell the children a traditional Christmas story.

CHAPTER 3

Mathematical development

The activities in this chapter will encourage children to develop their mathematical skills ranging from matching, ordering and recognizing numerals to counting, subtracting and using everyday words to describe position.

GROUP SIZE
Small groups.

TIMING
Ten to 15 minutes.

HOME LINKS
Send a note and diagram to parents and carers showing what you have been doing and how to make similar shape puzzles at home using old Christmas cards. Encourage them to work on jigsaw puzzles with their children and try out different types and shapes.

FIND THE MISSING SHAPE

Learning objective
To match shapes by recognizing similarities and orientation.

What you need
Six Christmas cards (large, colour pictures on cards of different shapes); scissors; sticky-backed plastic; A4 envelope; marker pen; ruler.

Preparation
Rule each Christmas card picture into two or three different shape pieces using a marker pen and cut out (see diagram). Number the back of each complete set of puzzle pieces with the same number. Store the pieces in an A4 envelope.

What to do
Mix up the puzzle pieces and place them all face upward in random order on one side of the table. Invite the children to look carefully at the pieces before asking a child to pick up one piece and to tell you what shape it is (rectangle, triangle). Ask the children if they can guess from this section what the whole picture will be. Talk about the different images to introduce Christmas vocabulary. Next, ask another child to look at similarities and differences on the other pieces to find a piece that goes with the first one. When a piece is selected, invite the child to tell you what shape the piece is and place it alongside the first piece. If the children are not sure if they have the correct piece, let them turn the piece over and check the numbers on the back.

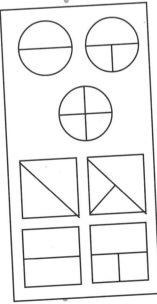

Use the correct names for the different shapes and encourage the children to do the same. When all the pieces have been found to make each puzzle, talk about the different pieces and how when they are put together they make up a whole picture.

Support
Limit the number of puzzles to just three for younger children.

Extension
Let older children make their own puzzles and increase the number of pieces that each puzzle is divided into.

Mathematical development

GROUP SIZE
Whole group for discussion; three children for activity.

TIMING
15 minutes.

WHICH TREE IS THE TALLEST?

Learning objective
To order items by length and to use language such as greater and smaller.

What you need
Three kitchen-roll tubes; green card; scissors; six squares of cardboard approximately 15cm x 15cm; stick-on Christmas shapes; brown and brightly-coloured paint; paintbrushes; wooden ruler; glue; spreaders; six egg-box lids; the photocopiable sheet on page 67; card; marker pen.

Preparation
Show the children how to paint the kitchen-roll tubes brown and egg-box lids in bright colours. When dry, cut each tube in half. Make two copies of the photocopiable sheet onto card. Cut out six Christmas tree shapes, two of each of the three sizes and decorate with the stick-on shapes. Cut a slit around the base of each tube and bend out before sticking one tree shape to each. Once the glue is dry, attach the tube to an egg-box lid ensuring that the tree stands straight and is stuck firmly. Write number '1' on the underside of the smallest tree lids, '2' on the middle-sized tree lids and '3' on the biggest tree lids to make two sets.

What to do
Talk to the children about size and how people are all different, as we are individuals. Ask four children to stand together in front of the others and point out how they are all different (remain sensitive to individuals). Stand with the four children and show that now you are the tallest. Explain that other people are taller than you.

Place one set of trees on the table and invite a child to pick up the smallest tree. Ask another child which tree is next in size and to place it alongside the first. Finally, ask another child to place the third tree in its correct position in order of size. Check if they are correct by turning each tree over and looking at the number that is written on the base. Stimulate discussion by asking 'Which tree is bigger/smaller than this one?'. Take the third tree away and ask which tree is now the biggest. Use mathematical language of small, smaller, smallest; big, bigger, biggest and encourage observational skills. Explain that the second tree is smaller than the third tree but bigger than the first.

Bring out the second set of trees and hold up each in turn to see if the children can find the matching tree on the table to the one you are holding.

Support
Focus on just one set of trees for younger children.

Extension
Show older children how to use a ruler to measure the different trees, providing close supervision.

HOME LINKS
Ask parents and carers to find opportunities for their children to look at differences in the size of people and items in their immediate environment. Stress the use of correct language.

Mathematical development

MY CHRISTMAS STOCKING

GROUP SIZE
Two children.

TIMING
Ten to 15 minutes.

Learning objective
To recognize numerals 1 to 9.

What you need
The photocopiable sheet on page 68; brightly-coloured pieces of card; scissors; bodkins; thick, glittery wool; cotton wool; sequins; stick-on shapes; containers; paper clips; glue; spreaders; hole-punch; marker pen; sticky tape; selection of Christmas stockings; pencil; glitter pens; shoelaces; number line; kitchen-roll tube; tissue paper.

Preparation
Copy the photocopiable sheet onto coloured card to make two in each colour. Use a paper clip to join two pieces the same colour together and punch holes where shown.

What to do
Display the children's Christmas stockings on a table and ask the children to study each one in turn looking for similarities and differences.

Invite two children to find a pair of stockings in the same colour. Show the children how to attach the two pieces together with a paper clip and give each child a threaded bodkin. Let older children thread their own. Start each child off by knotting one end of the wool and attaching this knot firmly to the back of the top 'stocking' with sticky tape under hole '1'. Stress the importance of following the numbers in the correct order and keep the number line close by for reference.

When the sewing is complete, cut off the excess wool and put the end inside the stocking under number '9'. Next, ask each child to decorate the side of their stockings using the materials provided, to cover the numbers, and show them how to stick a layer of cotton wool round the top. Encourage each child to write their name on their stocking in pencil and to go over this with a glitter stick. Once the glue has dried, ask each child to stuff some tissue paper into their stocking using the kitchen-roll tube to push it into the foot section. Place one kitchen-roll tube into each stocking before filling the spaces around the sides with tissue paper. Cut off any excess cardboard, then punch a hole through the top left-hand corner of the stocking and attach a shoelace to each one to create a loop. Place some sweets (see 'Christmas long ago' on page 39) in the kitchen-roll tube inside each stocking.

HOME LINKS
Ask parents and carers to play board games with their children, where numbers must be followed in sequence and to provide sewing kits to develop manual dexterity.

Support
Draw lines to link the numbers for younger children to follow.

Extension
Encourage older children to work independently to complete the whole task.

Mathematical development

GROUP SIZE
Three children.

TIMING
15 minutes.

HOME LINKS
Invite parents and carers to play other board games such as *Snakes and Ladders* at home with their children.

THE WAY TO BETHLEHEM

Learning objective
To count accurately to 6.

What you need
The photocopiable sheets on pages 69 and 70; A4 card; dice; three large buttons/counters; coloured pencil crayons; sticky-backed plastic; scissors; A4 envelope.

Preparation
Copy the photocopiable sheets onto card, colour in using the pencil crayons and cover with sticky-backed plastic. Cut the instruction cards carefully along the marked lines and place both the baseboard and cards inside the A4 envelope.

What to do
Place the baseboard and the instruction cards on a table and explain how to play the game. Place the three buttons/counters in the first square and tell the children that they are each a Wise Man looking for the stable. Let each child take a turn to throw the dice and move forward the number of spaces shown. Encourage the children to count out loud the number of dots on the dice and the number of spaces they move.

When a child lands on one of the hazards or short cuts, ask them to find the relevant instruction card and look at what they have to do, for example, if they land on the mountains, they have to go back two spaces (shown by '–2' on the card). Alternatively, if they land on the star square they can move forward '+2' spaces. Encourage the children to identify whether they must move back or forwards by identifying the '+' and '–' signs on the cards. While they are playing, ask the children to think of additional hazards and shortcuts that the Three Wise Men could have come across on their journey. The first 'Wise Man' to reach baby Jesus in the stable is the winner.

Support
Help younger children to count the dots on the dice and interpret the instruction cards.

Extension
Invite older children to help with the colouring of the baseboard and instruction cards.

Mathematical development

GROUP SIZE
Three children.

TIMING
15 minutes.

SORT THE DECORATIONS!

Learning objective
To sort and match items into different categories.

What you need
Box of assorted Christmas decorations; shoeboxes; pieces of card approximately 10cm x 5cm; marker pen; two tables.

What to do
Ask the children to look carefully at the decorations and to think of ways to sort them. Show the children the shoeboxes and explain that they must sort the decorations into different categories and place them in the shoeboxes. Invite them to sort the decorations into categories according to colour. While the children are sifting through the decorations, encourage them to talk about what they are doing, for example, ask if they can tell you something about the decoration that they are holding and if they can find another one in the same colour or size.

When all the decorations have been sorted into categories, empty each shoebox and look at the contents in order to discuss why the children grouped those decorations together. Ask the children to count the number of decorations in each group and write the number on a piece of card, which can be placed in front of each box. Ask which group has the most decorations by looking at the numbers, for example, 'We have more blue than red decorations and very few yellow ones'. Finally, place the boxes in correct numerical order.

Support
Limit the number of decorations to be sorted for younger children and make the differences obvious.

Extension
Encourage older children to think of further ways in which they can sort the decoration according to texture, type of decoration or size and provide items with subtle differences.

HOME LINKS
Suggest to parents and carers that they let their children sort items at home, such as clean washing or cutlery.

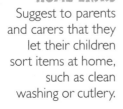

Mathematical development

GROUP SIZE
Whole group.

TIMING
Ten minutes.

COUNTDOWN TO CHRISTMAS

Learning objectives
To develop simple subtraction skills; to recognize number sequence.

What you need
White card approximately 60cm x 60cm; glue; spreaders; two A3 pieces of white card; scissors; glue stick; cotton-wool balls; stick-on circles; marker pen; pencil crayons; dinner plate; plastic lids approximately 2cm in diameter.

Preparation
Ask a child to trace around a dinner plate onto the square of card – this will be Santa's face. Draw a hat and facial features and decorate using the cotton wool, pencil crayons and stick-on circles. Next, invite each child to trace around a plastic lid onto one of the A3 pieces of card and to cut these circles out. Number the circles '1' to '24.' Ask the children to take turns sticking their circles in correct numerical order to form Santa's beard (see diagram left). Hang the Santa Advent calendar at child height where it will be easily accessible to the children at circle time.

What to do
Explain what Advent is, how it means 'The coming of Jesus Christ' and how we count the days until Christmas in this period. On the 1 December, ask the children to look carefully at the calendar and to tell you what number is first on Santa's beard. Invite a child to glue a piece of cotton wool over the '1' on the calendar. Repeat this the next day, giving another child a turn, and saying that we have taken away one day so which number is next in line? Before the child covers the number, ask them to tell you once again what the number is.

Once covered, ask them what the next number in the line will be. Repeat each day until all the numbers have been covered and Santa's beard is completely covered with 'hair' (cotton-wool balls).

Support
Help younger children to trace around the dinner plates and plastic lids and recognize the numbers.

Extension
Invite older children to count how many days are left on the calendar until Christmas after each day's number has been covered.

HOME LINKS
Ask parents and carers to provide an Advent calendar at home and to draw their children's attention to each number as it is revealed.

Mathematical development

GROUP SIZE
Whole group.

TIMING
15 to 20 minutes

PIN THE STAR ON THE TREE

Learning objective
To use everyday words to describe position.

What you need
Display board; length of non-fungicide wallpaper approximately 60cm x 60cm; photocopiable sheet on page 73; A4 gold and silver card; double-sided sticky tape; A3 sheet of paper; marker pen; pencil crayons; ruler; scissors; A4 envelope; shoebox; blindfold; pencil.

Preparation
Draw a Christmas tree on the length of wallpaper. Invite the children to colour it green and hang it on a display board. Make a chart on the A3 paper with the children's names down the left-hand side of the page and space to write in their measurement alongside it. Copy the photocopiable sheet onto gold or silver card and cut out a star template for each child. Attach a piece of double-sided sticky tape to the back of each one before placing in a shoebox!

What to do
Explain that each child is going to pin a star on the Christmas tree, without looking, to see who can get nearest to the top. Ask the children to take turns to take a star from the box, put on the blindfold and pin the star on the tree. Some children may not want to wear the blindfold, so don't force them but ask them to close their eyes. When the blindfold is removed (or eyes are opened) the children will have great fun seeing where their star has landed. Write the children's names in pencil on their star.

When all the children have had a turn ask them whose star they think is the closest to the top of the tree. Measure the distance from the top of the tree to the centre of each star to see whose star is in fact the closest. While you measure, say, for example, 'This star is 'further' away than this one' or 'This one is 'closer'' and so on using everyday words that the children are familiar with. Write down the measurement next to each child's name on the chart and hang the completed chart next to the tree.

Support
Encourage younger children to understand which star is nearer or further from the top of the tree, in terms which they can comprehend.

Extension
Invite older children to help record the measurements on the chart.

HOME LINKS
Ask parents and carers to talk to their children about distance while out walking, for example, 'We've only just left home' and a bit later 'We're nearly there now, we're getting closer'.

Mathematical development

GROUP SIZE
Two children.

TIMING
Ten to 15 minutes.

PRESENTS GALORE

Learning objective
To count reliably up to 10 everyday objects and to recognize numerals.

What you need
Twenty pieces of card approximately 2cm x 2cm; sticky-backed plastic; ten pieces of thick card approximately 30cm x 25cm; thin pieces of tinsel; two small boxes; hole-punch; old Christmas wrapping paper; marker pen; sticky tape.

Preparation
Write the numerals 1 to 10 on ten of the twenty pieces of card, and write either '=', '+' or '–' symbol on the remaining ten. Cover all the cards with sticky-backed plastic. Fold ten pieces of thick card in half and punch a hole at the top in the centre. Cut out pictures from old Christmas wrapping paper and stick one to the first card, two to the next and so on up to ten, leaving a space between each picture. Place the number cards in one small box and the number symbols in the other. Thread a piece of tinsel through the hole in the top of the card and stick down at the back with a piece of sticky tape.

What to do
Place the boxes with the number and symbol cards in the middle of the table along with the ten 'present' cards. Explain that each 'present' has a different amount of items on it and show the children how to move the tinsel around on the card to get different number combinations (see diagram). Invite each child to choose a 'present', place the tinsel in the centre, and count how many items in total are on their card. Encourage them to experiment by moving the tinsel to one side of their card and counting how many items on either side of the tinsel.

While the children are working, use language such as there are 'more' items on this side and 'less' this side and so on. Once the children are confident, ask them to find the correct numeral card, from the pile on the table, that represents the total number of items on their 'present' and to put it underneath their card. Next, they can place a number card under each side of the piece of tinsel. Show the children the maths symbols cards explaining that a ' + ' sign means add something and a '–' means take away with the ' = ' being the sum total.

HOME LINKS
Give parents and carers a copy of the photocopiable sheet on page 71 and ask them to help their children to complete it at home.

Support
Limit the 'present' cards to just three for younger children and slowly increase as the children's skills improve.

Extension
Encourage older children to use the maths symbol cards.

CHAPTER 4

Knowledge and understanding of the world

This chapter provides activities to encourage children to develop their knowledge and understanding of the world. They will be able to observe changes while cooking Christmas biscuits, make play-dough figures for a nativity scene and find out how Christmas was celebrated a long time ago.

GROUP SIZE
Two children.

TIMING
Ten to 15 minutes.

STAINED-GLASS WINDOW

Learning objective
To investigate objects and materials using different senses.

What you need
A window; soap flakes; wide masking tape; newspaper; medium and small paintbrushes; aprons; paint pots with lids; pictures of stained-glass windows; coloured and black paint.

Preparation:
Select a window where there is good light and space for the children to paint freely. Cover the floor with newspaper and have a bowl of clean water on hand. Mix coloured paint with some soap flakes that will help to thicken the paint and make it easier to wash off the window. Mark off small areas of the window using masking tape.

What to do
Look at pictures of stained-glass windows and during any visits to church (see 'Church outing' on page 13). Explain that in churches these normally depict the life of Jesus or another aspect of the bible.

Invite each child to put on an apron and to paint one section of glass between the masking tape lines with a medium-sized paintbrush using just one colour paint for each section. If you have sufficient window space, let each child paint another section. Encourage the children to talk about what they are doing and how it is different to paint on the window compared with painting on paper.

When all the children have had a turn, and the stained-glass window is complete, carefully remove the masking tape from between the painted sections. Next, invite the children to help paint in the 'leaded' sections with small paintbrushes using black paint.

Support
Help younger children to paint the 'leaded' sections as this requires more skilful hand co-ordination.

Extension
Ask older children to help mark off the areas to be painted.

HOME LINKS
Give parents and carers a copy of the photocopiable sheet on page 72 and ask them to help their children complete it at home.

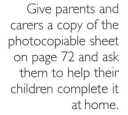

EARLY YEARS ACTIVITY CHEST Christmas activities

Knowledge and understanding of the world

GROUP SIZE
Two children.

TIMING
Ten to 15 minutes.

IT'S A WRAP

Learning objective
To look at patterns and change.

What you need
Coloured marbling paints; old square bowl; sheets of coloured paper; scissors; water; dowelling rod; glue; spreaders; pack of new pencil crayons; newspaper; aprons; pipettes; paper towels.

Preparation
Place a sheet of coloured paper underneath the bowl, trace around, remove the bowl and cut out the shape. Repeat to provide one sheet for each child. Cover the table with newspaper and place the bowl, full of water, in the centre.

What to do
Invite one child to choose a colour of marbling paint and to use a pipette to drop a small amount of paint onto the surface of the water. Ask the children to observe what happens and to comment as the paint hits the water. With the paint floating on top of the water, ask the child to take a dowelling rod and to swirl the paint around. Ask the second child to repeat the process, using another colour paint, and then invite both children to take turns to swirl the paint around.

Stimulate discussion by asking the children why they think the paint is floating on the water. Explain that the oil in the paint makes it float. When each child has made a pattern they like, ask them to pick up a sheet of paper and to gently place it on the surface of the water. Carefully, peel off the paper, allow the excess water to drip off, before placing on a flat surface to dry. Encourage the children to make further prints. Use the paper to decorate a new pack of pencil crayons by covering a plain pencil in glue and wrapping the marbled paper (cut to size) to it. Alternatively, use it as wrapping paper at Christmas time.

To clear the paint off the water for the next group of children, place a piece of paper towel over the paints and lift off. Explain to the children that the towel absorbs the paints.

HOME LINKS
Ask parents and carers to make a marbling paint with their children at home by mixing a small amount of cooking oil with food colouring.

Support
Work individually with younger children to help them achieve success.

Extension
Invite older children to make their own marbling paints by mixing cooking oil with powdered paint.

Knowledge and understanding of the world

GROUP SIZE
Five children.

TIMING
20 to 25 minutes.

EUROPEAN SPICY BISCUITS

Learning objective
To observe changes before and after cooking.

What you need
For the biscuits: 170g self-raising flour; 1 teaspoon ground ginger; 55g margarine; 70g golden syrup; 140g soft brown sugar; few teaspoons of water; ½ teaspoon mixed spice; ½ teaspoon bicarbonate soda; ½ teaspoon salt (to make 15 biscuits); food colouring; icing sugar; cherries; currants. Equipment: oven; microwave oven; measuring scales; teaspoons; sieve; rice paper; baking tray; mixing bowl; wire rack; greaseproof paper; Christmas shape cutters; rolling-pin; aprons; spatula; small bowls; blunt knives; clear plastic jug; wooden spoon; six small baking boards; tea towel; pen.

Preparation
Preheat the oven to 180°(350°F) or Gas Mark 4 and place a sheet of greaseproof paper on the baking tray. Cut the rice paper into squares and write each child's name on each one. Make up a few batches of icing sugar in different bowls, cover with a damp tea towel and place in a fridge. (NB Check for any food allergies and dietary requirements.)

What to do
Ask the children to wash their hands and to put on an apron. Work with the children to place all the 'dry ingredients' in a bowl, demonstrating how you measure out the ingredients using the scales. Place the syrup and margarine in a clear plastic jug and heat in a microwave (on a low power) until the margarine melts. Show the children the changes that have occurred and how the heat has made the margarine change from a solid into a liquid. Pour this mixture gradually into the dry mixture, stirring at first with a wooden spoon and then kneading the mixture with your hands until you have a smooth lump of dough. Add more water if the dough is too stiff or more flour if too sticky. Remove and place on a baking board before dividing into five equal ball sizes of dough.

Invite each child to make Christmas biscuits from the dough by rolling it out, not too thin, and cutting shapes using the cutters. Place the shapes onto the baking tray, labelling each child's biscuits with their name and cook for about ten minutes. Remove from the oven and place on a baking rack to cool. When the biscuits are cool ask the children to describe the texture and form of the biscuits which are now dry and hard following the cooking process. Ask each child to decorate their biscuits using the coloured icing sugar.

HOME LINKS
Give the recipe to parents and carers for them to make biscuits at home with their children.

MULTICULTURAL LINKS
Tell the children how different European countries make spicy biscuits as decorations, for example, German children make decorations for their Christmas trees and Norwegian children make gingerbread men and houses.

Support
Help younger children to roll out the dough to the correct thickness.

Extension
Encourage older children to remember the correct sequence of the recipe and to 'write' it on a piece of paper along with illustrations.

Knowledge and understanding of the world

GROUP SIZE
Two children.

TIMING
15 minutes.

STARS IN THE BETHLEHEM SKY

Learning objective
To investigate magnets and to find out how things work.

What you need
The photocopiable sheet on page 73; A4 pieces of gold and silver card; dark blue paint; paintbrushes; scissors; paper clips; sticky tape; roll of thick plastic; craft knife; two large magnets; large, stiff cardboard box; marking pen; small piece of fabric; plastic button.

Preparation
Cut off two of the opposite sides of a cardboard box, leaving two sealed sides, and ask the children to help you to paint it dark blue. Copy the stars on the photocopiable sheet onto gold and silver card to make ten and number them '1' to '10'. Attach a paper clip to the back of five stars, with sticky tape, and a piece of fabric, plastic button and so on to the other five stars. Stand the box on one of the closed sides and place the stars on the other closed side facing upwards. Cover the stars with a piece of thick plastic by loosely sticking it down underneath the top section of the box.

What to do
Invite two children to sit alongside the box and explain that in the Christmas story, the shepherds and the Wise Men had to find their way to Bethlehem by looking at the stars in the sky. Take one of the large magnets, place your hand under the top section of the box and move the magnet around. The children will soon realize that some of the stars move. Ask the children why they think this is happening. Invite them to move all the stars that will move to the top of the 'sky' and leave the ones that will not at the bottom.

Remove the plastic and ask the children to take off the stars at the top of the box and place them in one pile and the others, at the bottom of the box, in another pile.

Turn the stars over and show the children the backs of each one, explaining that the stars with the paper clip moved as the clip is made of iron, whereas the other stars had plastic or fabric on them which a magnet is not attracted to. Show this using the large magnet.

Finally, place the stars with the paper clips back in the sky and ask the children to move the stars around at their own will, from one side of the sky to the other.

Support
Limit the stars to no more than five for younger children.

Extension
Encourage older children to move a star with a number chosen by you or another child to the top of the 'sky'.

HOME LINKS
Ask parents and carers to collect some small objects that contain iron such as a paper clip, and others that do not such as a pencil crayon, and place them in a shoebox. Using a fridge magnet, they can invite their children to try to find the objects in the shoebox that contain iron and those that do not and to place them in separate piles.

Knowledge and understanding of the world

GROUP SIZE
Whole group.

TIMING
20 to 25 minutes.

HOME LINKS
Ask parents and carers of different nationalities if they could contribute a traditional food dish for the party or loan a traditional decoration.

LET'S PARTY

Learning objective
To find out about our own Christmas traditions and beliefs and those of other people.

What you need
Evergreen potted plant; pieces of card approximately 15cm x 6cm; yellow shredded tissue paper; white table-cloth; sponge cake; white icing sugar; water; container; tablespoon; spatula; cake decoration figure of Santa, trees and flowers; Christmas decorations; marker pen; white shirt; length of red tinsel; strip of white card approximately 13cm x 3cm; orange felt-tipped pen; paper plates; serviettes; blunt knife; scissors; stapler; A4 sheet of white card; mince pies; salad; cold meats.

Preparation
Ice the sponge cake and place a figure of Santa, some trees and flower decorations on top. Cut out four candles from white card and colour in a flame on each using an orange felt-tipped pen. Measure the white length of card around a child's head before stapling the two ends together and attach the four candles to the crown. Put a white cloth on the table and spread some shredded tissue paper on the floor around the table. Place all the food on the table and decorate the room. Write the name of each country represented on cards and place them in front of the food and decorations. (NB Be aware of any food allergies and dietary requirements.)

What to do
Write all the girls' names on separate pieces of paper and mix them together. Choose one to be 'Lucia' and dress her in a white shirt with the red tinsel sash wrapped around her waist and the candle crown on her head.

Explain to the children that most countries have their own traditional foodstuff and decorations relating to Christmas. Tell them that the child in white is dressed in the traditional clothes of a child in Scandinavia to celebrate the festival of St Lucia; the sponge cake is a traditional Japanese Christmas cake; the potted plant is a traditional Christmas tree of an Indian family and the straw under the table is how Polish people remember that Baby Jesus was born in a stable.

Talk to the children about countries such as Australia where it is hot and many people have their Christmas meal outside, which is often salad and cold meats. Tell the children that the mince pies are a traditional English treat and that the mincemeat represent spices from the East, a reminder of the Wise Men. Finally, invite the children to eat the food.

Support
Keep the discussion simple for younger children.

Extension
Older children can help to label the cards for the different countries.

Knowledge and understanding of the world

GROUP SIZE
Small groups.

TIMING
Ten to 15 minutes for preparation; ten to 15 minutes for activity.

HOME LINKS
Give parents and carers copies of the play dough recipe for them to make a batch with their children at home.

MULTICULTURAL LINKS
Add some other figures to the nativity scene such as a baker or butcher, which is a traditional French custom.

NATIVITY SCENE

Learning objective
To construct models using a range of materials and tools.

What you need
The photocopiable sheet on page 74; play dough; modelling tools; airtight container; cardboard box; shredded tissue paper; scrap pieces of fabric, braid, wool; display board; black paper; stick-on gold stars in different sizes; pipe-cleaners; shoebox; pieces of card approximately 7cm x 4cm; twigs; marker pen; craft knife; brown paint; tray; sand; rice; paintbrushes; glue; spreaders; matchbox (for crib); aprons; pieces of paper.

Preparation
Use the photocopiable sheet to make a batch of play dough Store in an airtight container. Use a craft knife to cut one of the ends off a cardboard box and make a window shape in two sides. Ask the children to help you paint it brown. Once the paint has dried, stick twigs onto the roof. Attach a piece of black paper to a display board and cover with stick-on gold stars. Stick a large gold star above the stable. Write the names of the figures in the nativity on a piece of paper and place in a shoebox.

What to do
Ask each child to take a piece of paper with the names of the figures on from the shoebox and explain that they will make that person/animal using the play dough and other materials. Show the children how to roll a piece of play dough into a shape, which will stand easily, and then encourage them to decorate as they wish. Use the modelling tools to make hair for the figures and fur for the animals. Use the material scraps for capes or head-dresses and the pipe-cleaners as a crook for the shepherds. Put rice in the play dough to make sheep. Encourage the children to talk about the difference in texture between the two types of play dough.

When the figures are complete, place them in the 'stable' or alongside it. Scatter some shredded tissue paper on the floor of the stable and place Baby Jesus in his 'crib'.

Support
Help younger children with the modelling of the figures as necessary.

Extension
Invite older children to help to make the labelling cards for the nativity scene and to put them in front of the various figures.

Knowledge and understanding of the world

GROUP SIZE
Whole group for discussion; small groups for activity.

TIMING
15 to 20 minutes.

CHRISTMAS LONG AGO

Learning objective
To find out about how Christmas was celebrated in the past.

What you need
The photocopiable sheet on page 75 and ingredients listed; pencil crayons; bowl for each child; spoon; plastic film covering; aprons; two hula hoops; two pieces of card approximately 30cm x 10cm; marker pen; paper decorations; apple or orange; knitted toy; wooden toy; home-made sweets; brightly-coloured decorations; modern toys; bags of sweets.

Preparation
Place the hula hoops on the floor with all the items, toys and decorations that relate to Christmas long ago, and all the modern ones in the other. Attach labels saying 'Christmas when Great-Grandma and Great-Grandad were young' and another saying 'Christmas today'.

What to do
Talk to the children about Christmas when their great-grandparents were young and how it was very different for children then. Explain that during the Second World War (1939–1945) it was not possible to buy many toys as the metal used for toys was needed for other things. Food was rationed and sweets and other such things were not available and people had to make their own.

Ask the children to look carefully at the items in the hoop with the label 'Christmas when Great-Grandma and Great-Grandad were young' such as the knitted toy, orange, wooden toy and paper decorations. Tell them that many parents made toys for their children and that each child would usually only receive one toy for Christmas. Children made their own paper decorations and instead of sweets, received either an apple or orange in their stocking. Compare the two groups of items and talk about how they are different. How would the children feel if they got the presents that are in their great-grandparents' hoop?

Finally, divide the children into smaller groups and, using the photocopiable sheet, make a simple sweet that would have been made during the war years. (NB Check for any food allergies and dietary requirements.) Place the sweets in the Christmas stocking made during the activity 'My Christmas stocking' on page 27.

HOME LINKS
Invite great-grandparents, grandparents or older relatives to come into your setting and to talk about their childhood Christmas experiences with the children.

Support
Have fewer items in each hoop for younger children.

Extension
Ask older children to look carefully at the items in each hoop in turn, look away and try to recall from memory what is in each one.

EARLY YEARS ACTIVITY CHEST Christmas activities

Knowledge and understanding of the world

GROUP SIZE
Whole group for discussion; individuals for use of tape recorder.

TIMING
Ten to 15 minutes.

HOME LINKS
Send a letter to parents and carers explaining what you have been doing and ask them to allow their child to use a tape recorder to 'interview' members of the family about what they would like for Christmas.

MY CHRISTMAS WISH

Learning objective
To use everyday technology to communicate.

What you need
Tape recorder; two A3 sheets of paper; marker pen; display board.

Preparation
Divide the A3 sheets of paper into squares, write each child's name down the left-hand side of the paper and leave a space where their thoughts can be recorded and illustrated. On the first sheet, write 'What I would like for Christmas' and on the second sheet, write 'What I would not like'.

What to do
Show each child how to use the tape recorder and explain why it needs batteries and a cassette in it so that it will work properly. Explain the 'play', 'off', 'forward' and 'rewind' buttons. Invite them to record a message saying what they would like for Christmas and what they would not like, rewind the tape, listen to it and re-record if they want to. When they are happy with their message, write their wish down in the column next to their name and what they would not like on the other sheet of paper. They can then draw a picture of these items next to the words.

When all the children have recorded their wishes, place the charts on the display board and ask them to come to sit with you. Invite each child to tell the others what they would like for Christmas, and why, by pointing to the chart next to their name and showing the words and picture. They can then tell the others what they would not like for Christmas and why. Ask the children what they would feel like if they received the present that they least wanted. While you are going through the messages, some of the items will appear again; see if the children notice this and can point out the words.

Support
Help younger children to use the tape recorder.

Extension
Older children could take turns to 'interview' each other and find out what each one would and would not like for Christmas. Play the tape back and see if the children can identify who is speaking.

CHAPTER 5

Physical development

The activities in this chapter are directed at children expanding their physical development with ideas such as pretending to be toys in Father Christmas' working, threading pasta onto ribbon to create Christmas garlands and making Christingles.

GROUP SIZE
Small groups.

TIMING
Ten to 15 minutes.

HOME LINKS
Ask parents and carers if they could take their children to a Christingle service at their local church which are often held on Christmas Eve.

MULTICULTURAL LINKS
Tell the children about the African harvest festival of Kwanzaa, which starts on the 26 December and lasts for seven days. Candles play an important role in this celebration as well and families light one candle each night over the seven days of the festival.

CHRISTINGLE

Learning objective
To handle a malleable material.

What you need
Potter's clay (non-firing); white candles; matchsticks; selection of seeds; small shells; aprons; pieces of red ribbon; containers; paint; paintbrushes; non-toxic varnish.

What to do
Ask the children if anyone has ever been to a Christingle service at their local church or knows what it is. Briefly explain that a Christingle means 'Christ light' and is a celebration of the coming of Jesus at Christmas, who is known as the light of the world. Invite each child to make a Christingle of their own. Ask the children to put on aprons and then give each child a piece of clay. Invite them to play with it, encouraging discussion about the texture and whether they like the feeling or not.

Ask each child to mould their piece of clay into a round ball shape that will stand easily on its own. Explain that the ball represents the world. Take one of the white candles to represent Jesus as the light of the world and push it firmly into the clay, making a hole. Remove the candle and encourage the children to decorate their clay balls using the shells and seeds, sticking them into the clay. Give each child another piece of clay and ask them to mould four small shapes from it. Next, insert a matchstick through the centre of each shape before pushing each stick firmly into the clay ball. Tell the children that these four sticks represent the four seasons and the small shapes represent food on earth. When the clay is dry, let the children paint and, in turn, varnish each Christingle and place the candles back in their holes. Finally, tie a piece of red ribbon round each one to represent Jesus' blood that is shed for us at Easter time.

Support
Help younger children to mould the clay into a ball shape.

Extension
Explain to older children in greater detail the religious significance of the different parts of the Christingle.

EARLY YEARS ACTIVITY CHEST Christmas activities

Physical development

GROUP SIZE
Two children.

TIMING
15 minutes.

LITTLE BABY JESUS

Learning objective
To handle tools and malleable materials with increasing control and co-ordination.

What you need
The photocopiable sheet on page 74; play dough; gold pipe-cleaners; cake decoration balls in a variety of colours; short red strips of angelica; rolling-pins; modelling tools; empty 250g rectangular margarine tubs; pastry boards; aprons; sticky tape; brown, yellow, white and black wool; brown sticky-backed paper; scissors.

Preparation
Using the photocopiable sheet, make three batches of play dough in very light yellow, brown and white. Cut the brown, black and yellow wool into short lengths.

What to do
Tell the children that they are going to make a baby Jesus in a crib. Ask them to put on aprons and show them how to cover a margarine tub with sticky-backed brown paper to make a 'crib'. Show them how to make a 'halo' to go over Baby Jesus' head by bending the top section of a gold pipe-cleaner into a circular shape and attaching the rounded piece to the rest of the pipe-cleaner. Stick the halo firmly to one end of the 'crib' using sticky tape. Now, ask each child to mould a baby Jesus using either the yellow or brown play dough, by rolling a sausage shape for the body and then a ball for the head. Explain that baby Jesus would have been wrapped in something called 'swaddling clothes' which is similar to a blanket. Show them how to make swaddling clothes by using a rolling-pin to roll out a piece of white play dough. Wrap this carefully around Baby Jesus leaving just the head exposed. Wrap a piece of white wool loosely around the swaddling clothes and tie together at the back.

Invite the children to choose the coloured cake decoration balls to make the eyes and to stick on a piece of angelica for a mouth. Make hair by placing a few short lengths of wool on the head and pressing firmly into the dough.

Finally, use the modelling tools and play dough to make a 'straw' lining for the crib to lay the baby on.

Support
Help younger children to roll out the play dough and stick the brown paper to the margarine tubs.

Extension
Invite older children to make additional figures to go alongside the crib.

HOME LINKS
Encourage parents and carers to let their children roll and cut out biscuit dough or pastry.

Physical development

GROUP SIZE
Two children.

TIMING
15 minutes.

GOLD AND SILVER GARLAND

Learning objective
To develop hand–eye co-ordination.

What you need
Containers; small bells; dry hollow pasta; lengths of thin coloured ribbon; bodkins; gold and silver card; the photocopiable sheet on page 73; gold and silver spray paint; newspaper; marker pen; scissors; pieces of card approximately 15cm x 10cm.

Preparation
Spray paint the pasta, half of them gold and the other half silver. Copy the stars on the photocopiable sheet onto gold and silver card and cut them out. Draw simple patterns, using the available items, on the pieces of card for the children to follow and place in a container.

What to do
Talk to the children about what a pattern is and what this means. Show them by placing a piece of pasta, a bell, a piece of pasta and a bell on the table and pointing out the pattern. Repeat, with different items and ask the children to point out the pattern, starting with the item on the left and finishing with the item on the right.

Next, let each child choose a length of ribbon, thread their bodkin and tie a large knot at one end. Ask each child to choose one pictorial pattern card from the container and to tell you what the pattern is. Next, tell them to thread the correct items onto their piece of ribbon following the pattern on the card. Repeat the pattern until the ribbon is full, ensuring that they end with the correct item. While the children are working, ask questions about what they are doing such as 'What is the next item you are going to thread?', 'What have you just threaded?' and so on.

When the children have finished, help them to tie a knot at the end of the ribbon and hang their patterns up to display them. Let the children take the garlands home so that they can put them on their Christmas trees.

Support
Help younger children to thread the items and tie the knots.

Extension
Invite older children to make up their own pictorial charts for other children to follow.

HOME LINKS
Invite parents and carers to draw their children's attention to patterns in their immediate environment such as on curtains or carpets.

Physical development

GROUP SIZE
Small groups.

TIMING
20 minutes.

HOME LINKS
Ask parents and carers to write different actions on pieces of paper, for example, asking their children to walk slowly to the bathroom, tiptoe to the kitchen and march around the bedroom.

FOLLOW THAT STAR!

Learning objective
To move with control and co-ordination.

What you need
The photocopiable sheets on pages 73 and 76; double-sided tape; gold and silver card; scissors; whistle; sheet of white A4 card; glue; spreader; sticky-backed plastic; 'crib' and 'baby Jesus' (see 'Little baby Jesus' on page 42); a small basket.

Preparation
Copy the photocopiable sheet on page 73 onto gold and silver card to make five gold and five silver stars and cut them out. Number each star '1' to '10' and evenly space out the stars across the room, starting with number '1'. Place the crib at the end of the trail after number '10'. Secure the stars firmly to the floor using double-sided tape. Copy the photocopiable sheet on page 76 onto card, cut out the six pictures and cover with sticky-backed plastic.

What to do
Ask the children to take off their shoes and socks and to stand next to star number '1'. Explain that they need to follow the footpath of stars until they reach star number '10', which is where baby Jesus is sleeping. Let each child step carefully from star to star, saying each number as they move, until they reach baby Jesus. Stress that they must look where they are going and try to stay on the stars without stepping off.

When they have achieved this, ask them to return to star number '1', explaining that there are more ways to get to Bethlehem than by just walking. This time invite each child in turn to select one of the action cards which will tell them how they have to move to Bethlehem, for example, they must jump from star to star or tiptoe. Encourage each child to read aloud which action is on their card before moving off to follow the stars to Bethlehem. Let each child reach Bethlehem before the next child takes their turn. Repeat, letting each child choose a different card.

Support
Help younger children to 'read' what is written on their card.

Extension
Encourage older children to think of additional ways of getting to Bethlehem.

Physical development

GROUP SIZE
Whole group.

TIMING
15 to 20 minutes.

FATHER CHRISTMAS' WORKSHOP

Learning objective
To move confidently and imaginatively with increasing control and co-ordination.

What you need
A large open space; the photocopiable sheet on page 57.

What to do
Ask the children to sit down and then read them the story 'Eric's Christmas toys' on the photocopiable sheet. Tell them that they are going to pretend to be toys in Father Christmas' workshop on Christmas Eve and stress that they must take care to move safely. Ask the children to take off their shoes and socks. Explain that the workshop is full of toys and demonstrate how each moves in turn.

Aeroplane: put out your arms to the sides and fly around the room, first in one direction and then the opposite way. Invite the children to copy you and encourage them to use the available space.

Clockwork toy soldier: show how to stand up tall and straight with your head held high, then turn the key in your side before marching around the room, left, right, left, right, in a straight line.

Dancing doll: hold your arms up high above your head and swirl around the room on tiptoes making sure that you do not knock into anyone.

Ice skates: put them on your feet and go sliding round and round the room.

Electric train: go slowly around the track moving your arms backwards and forwards, slowly, slowly, then faster, faster, round and round the track 'chook, chook'.

Jack-in-the-box: crouch down low in your box carefully closing the lid, sit quietly for a few seconds before jumping up out of the box as quickly and as high as you can.

To finish, explain that it's nearly time for Father Christmas to leave so you must help him pack up the toys by placing them carefully in his black bag and putting them in his sleigh.

Support
Encourage younger children to copy your movements.

Extension
Ask older children to think of additional toys and to suggest suitable actions for them.

HOME LINKS
Ask parents and carers to encourage their children to choose a toy at home and pretend to move like it.

MULTICULTURAL LINKS
Tell the children the different names given to Father Christmas in other countries, for example, in Holland and Sweden he is Saint Nicholas, in Italy she is La Befana and in Germany the Christkindel delivers presents.

Physical development

GROUP SIZE
Three children.

TIMING
Ten to 15 minutes.

HOME LINKS
Ask parents and carers to let their children practice throwing crumpled pieces of paper into an empty waste-paper basket from a set distance.

CHRISTMAS WREATH TARGET

Learning objective
To practice hand–eye co-ordination.

What you need
Large cardboard box; green and red tissue paper; craft knife; sticky tape; scissors; permanent marker pen; glue; spreaders; nine satin non-breakable Christmas decoration balls; A4 sheets of paper; basket; small white stick-on labels.

Preparation
Cut off the inner and outer flaps from one side of a large box ensuring the other end is securely closed. Stand the box on its open end and draw a large circle, the size of a dinner plate, in the centre of one side and cut out using the craft knife. Draw a second circle shape around the cut-out circle. Invite the children to crumple up pieces of red and green tissue paper and fill in the circle outline. Number stick-on labels 1 to 3 to provide three sets and stick one set to each group of coloured balls before placing them in a basket. Write each of the children's names down one side of the paper so that their scores can be recorded. Place the box in an open area and put the basket and balls approximately three metres away, behind a line drawn on the floor where the children must stand.

What to do
Ask the children to each choose one set of balls. Encourage each child to take a turn throwing each of their balls at the wreath taking careful aim at the hole before throwing. Balls that miss the target must be left where they land until all the children have taken their turn.

When all three children have had a turn, empty the balls out of the box. Encourage each child to pick up their own set of balls and to count how many went through the hole. Record the results on a chart alongside each child's name. Repeat, this time changing balls with another child. Finally, at the end of the activity add up the grand total of how many balls each child got through the wreath.

Support
Let younger children start from a distance of just two metres and slowly increase as their throwing skills improve.

Extension
Invite older children to think of other ways to throw the balls such as underhand or overhand and so on.

Physical development

GROUP SIZE
Eight children.

TIMING
15 minutes.

IN AND OUT THE SNOWMEN!

Learning objective
To negotiate a pathway.

What you need
Six identical empty juice bottles with lids; whistle; A5 pieces of coloured card; sand; funnel; scissors; glue; spreaders; pencil crayons; coloured stick on dots; six cardboard circles approximately 6cm in diameter; white paper; piece of white chalk; white paint; paintbrushes.

Preparation
Wash the bottles thoroughly and ask the children to help to paint them white. Draw faces on the six cardboard circles and when the paint on the bottles is dry, remove the lids and use the funnel to half-fill each with sand. Glue each bottle's lid in place before attaching a cardboard face to each one. Finally, ask the children to decorate the 'snowmen' using the card to make hats, stick on labels for buttons and so on.

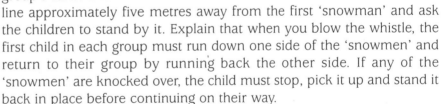

What to do
Divide the children into two teams of four and place three 'snowmen' approximately one metre apart in each group's lane. Draw a chalk line approximately five metres away from the first 'snowman' and ask the children to stand by it. Explain that when you blow the whistle, the first child in each group must run down one side of the 'snowmen' and return to their group by running back the other side. If any of the 'snowmen' are knocked over, the child must stop, pick it up and stand it back in place before continuing on their way.

Once the child has crossed the line to return (and sit down) the next child in the group starts. The group who are all sitting down with all the 'snowmen' still standing are the winners.

Support
Begin with just two snowmen for younger children.

Extension
Ask older children to run to the first 'snowman', pass to the right of it, the left of the second snowman and the right of the last one. They must then turn round and come back the same way until they reach their group. Explain that this is called a 'figure of eight' and help them to recognize the pattern by drawing it on the ground between the 'snowmen' using white chalk.

HOME LINKS
Invite parents and carers to set up a similar course at home by placing empty tins evenly spaced in the garden for their children to move around.

Physical development

GROUP SIZE
12 children.

TIMING
Ten to 15 minutes.

ON OUR WAY TO BETHLEHEM

Learning objective
To work as part of a team to move with confidence and in safety.

What you need
Four sheets of white A4 card; gold A4 card; four shoeboxes; Christmas wrapping paper; sticky tape; scissors; the photocopiable sheets on pages 73 and 77; doll; cardboard box; tissue paper; whistle; four dowelling rods approximately 15cm long; masking tape.

Preparation
Copy the photocopiable sheet on page 77 onto each of the four sheets of white card and cut out. Cover the four shoeboxes in Christmas wrapping paper. Copy the photocopiable sheet on page 73 onto gold card, cut out the stars and attach a dowelling rod firmly to the back of each one using sticky tape. Place the tissue paper into the cardboard box (crib) and place the doll (baby Jesus) on top. Mark out a start and finish line and four separate lanes using masking tape and place the 'crib' at the finish line. Place one of the stars in each of the four lanes approximately two metres from the start, then the presents, stars and sheep evenly spaced towards the finishing line.

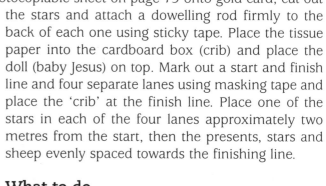

What to do
Divide the children into four groups of three and explain to them that the first group of children to reach baby Jesus, carrying the items collected in the correct order will be the winners. Emphasize the need for safe movement.

Blow the whistle and tell the first child in each group to run to the star in their lane, pick it up and return to their group with it. When this child crosses the line back at their group, they must take their place behind the third child (still holding their star). The second child now runs to one of the presents in their lane, picks it up and returns to their group, taking their place behind the first child. The third child then runs to the sheep, picks it up and returns to their group. Once this child has taken their place at the back of the group, the first child will be at the front of the line again, holding their star. This child must then 'light the way to Bethlehem' for the others by leading them the rest of the way. All the children must run together, staying behind the first child, in their correct order and still carrying their items until they reach 'Bethlehem'.

The group who cross the line first must place all their items alongside baby Jesus' crib, and sit down to win.

Support
Limit the number of groups to just two for younger children.

Extension
Encourage the children to play the game independently with minimum adult input.

HOME LINKS
Give parents and carers a copy of the photocopiable sheet on page 78 and ask them to help their children complete it at home.

CHAPTER 6

Creative development

The following activities concentrate on the area of creative development. Children will enjoy making a Rudolph reindeer puppet, designing a zigzag nativity book and creating musical instruments from different materials.

GROUP SIZE
Small groups.

TIMING
Ten to 15 minutes.

HOME LINKS
Invite parents and carers to tell their children a story about Rudolph the red-nosed reindeer, or sing a Christmas song and use the puppets as props.

MULTICULTURAL LINKS
Tell the children that in other countries, Father Christmas' sleigh is pulled by other animals, for example, in Sweden his sleigh is drawn by mountain goats, and in Holland St Nicholas delivers presents riding a horse.

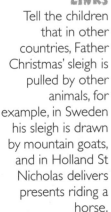

RUDOLPH REINDEER PUPPET

Learning objective
To make a construction using cutting and sticking techniques.

What you need
Pieces of brown and beige A4 card; scissors; red pom-poms; large black buttons; aprons; triangle template; sticky tape; pencil crayons; lolly sticks; glue; spreaders.

Preparation
Use a triangle template to draw on the sheets of brown cardboard to provide two triangles for each child.

What to do
Invite the children to put on an apron before sitting with them at the table. Ask who has heard of Rudolph the red-nosed reindeer. Tell the children that he is Father Christmas's favourite reindeer and is known for his bright red nose.

Explain to the children that they are going to make a Rudolph stick puppet. Give each child two pieces of brown card with the triangle marked on and ask them to cut these out. Next, invite each child to trace around their hands onto a piece of A4 beige cardboard and to cut out two handprints. Show them how to stick the handprints (antlers) behind one of the triangle shapes, along the longest edge. Turn the triangle over and stick a lolly sticky on the back of the shape, at the point opposite (see diagram) using a piece of sticky tape. The second triangle should then be stuck on top of this so that the lolly stick and glued 'antlers' are no longer visible. Finally, turn the triangle over and invite each child to decorate their Rudolph puppet using the materials provided such as a red pom-pom for a red nose and black buttons for eyes.

Support
Help younger children to trace around their hands and cut out the prints.

Extension
Encourage older children to trace around the triangle template themselves.

EARLY YEARS ACTIVITY CHEST Christmas activities

Creative development

GROUP SIZE
Whole group divided into groups of three or four children.

TIMING
15 to 20 minutes for each part.

CHRISTMAS WONDERLAND

Learning objective
To explore shape, colour, space and texture in three dimensions.

What you need
Pine cones; silver foil; circular piece of cardboard; plastic animals, cars and people; glue; spreaders; cardboard boxes in different shapes and sizes; small twigs; brown, green white and coloured paint; paintbrushes; wooden cotton reels; small coloured tissue-paper squares; silver and coloured glitter; cotton wool; clean, white sand; sand tray; scissors; containers; coloured stick-on dots; dead matchsticks; clean, empty milk carton.

Preparation
Fill the sand tray with clean, white sand. Cut the tissue-paper squares into small shapes.

What to do
Ask each child to choose something to make for the Christmas scene.
Christmas trees – mix glue and paint together and paint pine cones green, then sprinkle glitter on while still wet. Stick the trees to a wooden cotton reel that can also be painted.
Buildings – use the boxes to make a variety of buildings. Sprinkle silver glitter over the finished buildings and stick small coloured stick-on dots on some to look like Christmas lights. Add cotton wool to look like snow.
Church – stick an empty milk carton to another box, make a cross by attaching two matchsticks to the top of the church and add stained-glass windows by sticking small pieces of tissue paper to the sides of the box.
Frozen lake – stick a piece of silver foil to a piece of cardboard.
Trees – paint twigs brown and push them into the holes in the wooden cotton reels to be winter trees. Add cotton wool to look like snow.
Snowmen – stick two balls of cotton wool together and decorate as required.

HOME LINKS
Ask parents and carers to draw their children's attention to their immediate environment while out walking or driving during Christmas.

When the items are all dry, ask the children to suggest where they are going to place each item in the sand tray. Invite them to make roads in the sand alongside the 'buildings' before placing the plastic animals, cars and animals among the other seasonal items.

Support
Work with no more than two or three younger children at a time.

Extension
Encourage older children to help with smaller details such as sticking on the coloured dots which requires more fine motor control.

Creative development

GROUP SIZE
Two or three children.

TIMING
15 to 20 minutes.

ALL KINDS OF ANGELS

Learning objective
To work creatively on a small scale.

What you need
The photocopiable sheet on page 58; strong glue; spreaders; gold and silver doilies; gold and silver pipe-cleaners; kitchen-roll tubes; wooden cotton reels; scissors; A4 sheets of paper; gold and silver pine cones painted during the activity 'Gold and silver garland' on page 43; ping-pong balls; gold and silver tinsel; aprons; lengths of yellow, brown and black wool; containers; stick-on dots; white paint, paintbrushes; permanent marker pen; corrugated white cardboard.

Preparation
Cut the wool into short lengths and the doilies and kitchen-roll tubes in half. Ask the children to help you to paint the kitchen-roll tubes and wooden cotton reels white.

What to do
Read the poem on the photocopiable sheet about the angel who is different and when you have finished encourage the children to discuss it. Explain that everyone is an individual and that no two people are ever completely the same as each other.

Invite the children to choose any item from the materials available as a body for their angel (this could be either the kitchen-roll tube, a pine cone or wooden cotton reel). Ask them to find a head for their angel such as a ping-pong ball or a second pine cone. Encourage the children to experiment with different combinations and ideas until they have decided on their angel. Attach each head to the angel's body with glue and let the children decorate using the materials provided.

Suggest that the children make hair from wool and draw a face on the ping-pong ball, or stick on dots attached to a pine cone. Show them how to make halos by winding a pipe-cleaner or piece of tinsel around the angel's head. Wings can be made using half a doily, a piece of corrugated cardboard or white paper cut into a wing shape. Wrap an entire pipe-cleaner around the back of each pine cone to form arms. Help the children to decide what they need as necessary, stressing that there is no right or wrong way to make their angels.

Support
Help younger children to fix together their angels.

Extension
Ask older children to think of other materials which would be suitable to make an angel.

HOME LINKS
Encourage parents and carers to look at different angel decorations in shops and point out to their children how many there are to choose from, as people have different tastes and therefore will choose different angels.

Creative development

GROUP SIZE
Two children.

TIMING
15 minutes.

CHRISTMAS DRAWING BOXES

Learning objective
To respond individually to music.

What you need
Tape recorder; selection of fast and slow Christmas music; foil in different colours; four large, shallow baking trays; fork; old combs; pencil crayons; dowelling rods; A4 pieces of cardboard; aprons; fine white sand.

Preparation
Line each baking tray with a different-coloured piece of foil. Divide the sand into two piles, dampening half. Cover the foil in the base of two trays with damp sand, about ½cm in depth, and the other two trays with dry sand, which should then be smoothed down well. Cut the cardboard to form a few combs with interesting teeth patterns (see diagram).

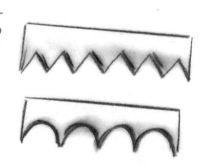

What to do
Ask each child to put on an apron and provide them with one tray of dry sand and one of damp sand each. Invite them to experiment freely with the two types of sand using the various tools, fork, pencil and so on. While the children are working, ask them to compare the patterns made using the different tools and ask which is their favourite tool and why. Draw their attention to the various patterns and designs created and how the foil in the base of the tray shows through, creating even more unusual designs. Ask them to try moving their hands up and down or even from side to side to see what patterns they can create. Encourage the use of words such as 'curved', 'pattern', 'squiggly' and 'pattern'.

Next introduce the Christmas music. As the music plays, encourage the children to listen and to make patterns in the sand reflecting how the music makes them feel. Make it clear that there is no right or wrong interpretation. Change the music at regular intervals, letting the children either flatten the sand and start over with new patterns, or continue their patterns. Ask the children to draw according to the tempo of the music, for example, with fast music to make patterns quickly and when the music is slow to slow down again. Finally, ask the children which sand they preferred drawing in and why.

HOME LINKS
Ask parents and carers to encourage their children to draw pictures while they listen to music and to talk about how the music makes them feel.

Support
Introduce younger children to the damp and dry sand at different times.

Extension
Encourage older children to draw a pattern in the sand for the other children to copy.

Creative development

GROUP SIZE
Two children.

TIMING
15 to 20 minutes.

ZIGZAG NATIVITY BOOK

Learning objective
To use folding and drawing skills.

What you need
Sheets of coloured and white A4 paper; glue; spreaders; the photocopiable sheet on page 79; sticky tape; pencil crayons; scissors; aprons.

Preparation
Copy the photocopiable sheet onto white A4 paper for each.

What to do
Ask each child to choose two pieces of coloured paper and fold them in half. Open up again and stick them securely together down the fold using a piece of sticky tape; for added strength place a second strip of sticky tape down the back of the paper. Now, fold the first sheet inwards to the join, the second sheet backwards and the last fold inwards.

Give each child a copy of the photocopiable sheet and ask them to colour in the pictures and to cut them out. Invite them to look carefully at each picture to decide the correct order of the story. When they are happy that they have the pictures in the correct order, open up the blank 'books' and invite them to stick their pictures on one side of the pages, from left to right, in the correct sequential order.

Once complete, ask each child to use crayons to add further details around the pictures such as animals around the crib and so on. Encourage them to complete the books by drawing a picture of their favourite part of the nativity story on the front cover and adding their names. Finally, ask the children to number the pages and then to 'read' the nativity story in the correct order.

Support
Help younger children to fold the paper. Talk through the sequence of the story with them, inviting them to pick the appropriate pictures in turn.

Extension
Let older children make a group zigzag nativity book containing pictures drawn by everyone. They must decide how many pages the book will have, how many drawings they will need, who will draw what and the correct sequential order of the pages.

HOME LINKS
Send a letter to parents and carers explaining how to make a simple zigzag book. Ask them to encourage their children to draw pictures of their own Christmas day in the book in the correct sequential order.

EARLY YEARS ACTIVITY CHEST Christmas activities

Creative development

GROUP SIZE
Small groups.

TIMING
15 minutes.

HOME LINKS
Suggest that the children investigate items at home which make a sound.

MULTICULTURAL LINKS
Talk to the children about traditional instruments in other cultures, for example, explain how a drum is very important in African cultures. Make a simple drum by covering the top of a round margarine tub with wax paper and securing it firmly around the sides with sticky tape.

CHRISTMAS BAND

Learning objective
To make musical instruments and show an interest in how they sound.

What you need
Tambourine; maracas; castanets; empty yoghurt pots; stones; lentils; glue; spreaders; bodkins; lengths of thin coloured ribbon; paint; sticky tape; paper plates; small bells; plastic and metal bottle caps; small tissue-paper shapes and other stick on shapes; hole-punch; aprons; thick card.

Preparation
Place all the instruments on a display table and the other materials on a separate table. Cut the thick card into pieces measuring approximately 15cm x 15cm.

What to do
Invite the children to investigate the tambourine, maracas and castanets encouraging them to talk about the shapes, how they feel and the different sounds that they make. Using these instruments as examples, ask each child what sort of instrument they would like to make. Urge them to look carefully at the materials offered and to decide what they will need to make the instruments.

Tambourines – stick two paper plates together and punch a series of holes, approximately 5cm apart, around the rims. Thread bottle caps and small bells onto lengths of thin ribbon using a bodkin and tie these securely from the holes in the paper plate.

Castanets – fold a strip of firm cardboard in half and glue a metal bottle cap on the inside of the two pieces.

Maracas – fill an empty yoghurt pot with a few stones or lentils. Place a second yoghurt pot on top of the other one, open ends together, and seal together tightly with sticky tape.

Provide support as the children make the instruments, helping them to experiment to achieve the best results. Let the children decorate the finished instruments, using the collage materials provided. Invite them to compare the sounds that their instruments make to those on display. Let the children use the made instruments to accompany any singing sessions (see 'Christmas carollers' on page 22).

Support
Limit the number of instruments and choice of materials offered for younger children.

Extension
Encourage older children to think of additional instruments they could make using the materials available.

Creative development

GROUP SIZE
Two children.

TIMING
15 minutes.

CRACKER CHRISTMAS CARDS

Learning objective
To make a three-dimensional structure.

What you need
Kitchen-roll tubes; glue; spreaders; coloured glitter; crêpe paper squares; stick-on foil shapes; glitter; sequins; non-fray plain fabric; pieces of braid; pinking shears; thick A4 coloured card; aprons; white paper approximately 10cm x 10cm; marker pen; felt-tipped pens; containers.

Preparation
Cut the kitchen-roll tubes in halves and then again lengthwise. Write short Christmas greetings on the pieces of paper such as 'Happy Christmas' or 'Merry Christmas'.

What to do
Ask each child to put on an apron, choose a piece of thick A4 coloured card and to fold it in half lengthwise. Look at the Christmas greetings together and ask if anyone recognizes any of the words. Help the children to read them out to you, pointing to the words in turn.

Ask each child to choose a message and to write it carefully on the inside of their card using the felt-tipped pens. Encourage them to cover one of the halved kitchen-roll tubes with a piece of fabric. Ensure that the whole tube is covered with glue so that the fabric will stick to it and make sure that the loose ends are tucked inside the back section of the tube. Stick each tube securely in the centre of each card. Now, encourage the children to decorate their card and cracker using the sequins, glitter, foil stick-on squares and so on. Show them how the braid can be stuck around the edges of the card to make a border. Stick a square of crêpe paper in each end of the cracker, pushing well into the hole, and use pinking shears to cut the end of each piece of crêpe paper to create a ruffle effect.

Support
Help younger children to write the Christmas message in their cards.

Extension
Encourage older children to look through old Christmas cards and to copy out a message from one of them.

HOME LINKS
Invite parents and carers to let their children look at Christmas cards received at home and to try to pick out words that they recognize in the greetings.

Creative development

GROUP SIZE
Four children.

TIMING
15 to 20 minutes.

A WISE MAN

Learning objective
To explore texture, colour, form and shape in three dimensions.

What you need
The photocopiable sheet on page 80 and items listed; biscuits; cherries; angelica; coconut; silver balls; four pastry boards; rolling-pins; aprons; icing sugar; small bowls; teaspoons; tray; small pieces of card; pen; two plastic bags; tray; pictures of the 'Three Wise Men'.

Preparation
Make a batch of candy clay in three colours and scents before placing in three containers. Put a small amount of coconut in a plastic bag, add a small amount of red food colouring, shake the bag and place the coloured coconut in a bowl to dry. Repeat with the green food colouring. Make up a bowl of white, red and green icing sugar. Write each child's name on a name card and place on the table.

What to do
Ask the children to wash their hands and put on an apron. Give each child a pastry board. Look at the pictures of the 'Three Wise Men' and point out how their clothes were different to ours. Ask each child to choose two balls of candy clay and to model a 'wise man' with it. As they mould the clay, talk about the texture and how it makes them feel. Encourage the children to use the ingredients to make a crown and so on for their figures. Talk about how the clay changes shape and takes form when it is moulded. Do any of the children notice the different smells of the different-coloured clay? Explain that the smells relate to the colours.

When the children have finished the modelling, show them how to mount each figure on a biscuit, using icing sugar. The base of the biscuit can also be covered with coloured coconut. Put the figures on a tray and ask each child to find their name label to place beside their models.

Support
Work with no more than two or three younger children at a time.

Extension
Encourage older children to try to recall the ingredients needed for the candy clay.

HOME LINKS
Give parents and carers a copy of the recipe on the photocopiable sheet so that they can make the candy clay with their children at home.

MULTICULTURAL LINKS
Explain to the children that in some countries the Three Wise Men play an important role, for example, in Italy children have to wait until 'Twelfth night' (6 January) to receive their presents as this is when the Three Wise Men arrived in Bethlehem with their gifts for Jesus.

Eric's Christmas toys

Eric the elf whistled as he skipped into the toy workshop. It was the week before Christmas, Eric's favourite time of the year.

All year long Eric and his friends worked hard, making toys for Father Christmas to deliver to children all over the world. There was no time for fun. They had too much to do. But the week before Christmas, Father Christmas asked each elf to choose toys to test, before they were wrapped and loaded into his sleigh. All week long, the elves played with the toys making sure that they were working just as they should. And Eric had chosen some really special toys this year.

First, he wound up a clockwork soldier. Left, right! Left, right! It waddled across the workbench. Eric tried to copy the funny walk. He was so busy trying to keep time, he didn't notice that it was getting near the edge of the bench. He only just managed to catch it, before it toppled onto the floor.

The aeroplane was next. Eric held it up above his head, pulled his arm back, and sent it zooming across the toyshop. It looped and swooped and glided down to land just in front of a twirling, dancing doll.

'Hey!' yelled the elf that was checking the doll. 'Careful!'

Eric thought he'd better try something else. He picked up a brightly-coloured box and pressed the button on it. 'Boing!' The lid flew open and up popped a smiling clown's face. The jack-in-the-box threw his arms up into the air. Eric jumped back in surprise.

'That's really fun!' he thought. He crept up behind his friend, Eddie.

'Boo!' he shouted, leaping up into the air. 'I'm a jack-in-the-box!'

'You're a nuisance!' laughed Eddie. 'You nearly made me drop this toy car.'

'Sorry!' mumbled Eric.

He wandered back to his toys. The electric train was next on his list. He was looking forward to this one! He set it off along the track. 'Clickety-clack! Clickety-clack!' It got faster and faster. Eric ran round the bench, trying to keep up with it. This train was fantastic.

'Woo! Woo!' he called in excitement.

'Excuse me!' said Ernie, one of the quieter elves. 'I'm trying to test this board game. Can you make less noise, please?'

Eric blushed. 'Of course,' he said, reaching across his workbench to pick up a large box.

He had one last thing to check. He put his hand into the box and pulled out a pair of shiny new skates. He slipped out through the door into the cold winter air. At the back of the workshop was a large pond, frozen over with thick ice.

Eric pushed his feet into the skates and stepped onto the pond. He glided to and fro, round and round. The skates worked really well. Eric smiled.

This would be a wonderful Christmas. He had enjoyed every one of the toys that he had tried, and he was sure that the children who got them as presents would love them, too.

Jillian Harker

The angel who is different

The Angel who
Does not sing or fly
Sits alone on her cloud
And she watches the sky.

She has two Angel wings
Of a snowy-white down
With a halo of gold
And a flowing white gown.

She finds it so peaceful
Up there on her cloud;
She's more happy *alone*
Than she is in a crowd.

For the Angel who
Does not sing or fly,
Writes *wonderful* stories —
And
    paints THE SKY!

Trevor Harvey

Welcome Baby Jesus

Opening scene: A newspaper stand poster saying 'Comet from the East to pass over Britain'. Narrator picks up a paper and begins to read.

Narrator: Wise Astronomers have been following a large comet travelling around the world. It will pass over the north of England very soon. Many people hoping to see it are travelling to a small village in the Lake District.

Mary and Joseph enter. Joseph appears to be driving a car. Mary is map reading.

Joseph: Not far now, Mary. Oh no! The car has broken down!

Narrator: The car cannot be mended, so Mary and Joseph decide to walk into the village. Joseph asks at a hotel for a room for the night, but they are fully booked. It is the same everywhere....

Hotel receptionist: Sorry we are full up. Everyone has come to see the comet.

Mary: I am very tired.

Narrator: Mary and Joseph are told that a farm outside the village does bed and breakfast, but when they arrive, it too, is full. The farmer suggests that they sleep in his barn. During the night Mary's baby is born. In the hills around the village, farmers and shepherds in small cottages are woken by the voices of angels singing about a baby.

Angels enter and with others on stage, sing a carol. When they go outside, the sky is full of bright light.

Shepherd/farmers: It's the comet. Look, it has stopped over the old barn!

Narrator: Down in the valley, the comet is low in the sky over the barn. Everywhere is peaceful and wonderful. Birds and animals move gently down the hills to be near the barn, and the shepherds and farmers follow them, taking small gifts for the baby. They are not afraid, but full of happiness. The astronomers arrive by helicopter and they are astonished to find that the comet has stopped. They are told about the baby.

Wise Astronomers: How could a comet stop like this? It must be a very special baby.

Narrator: Quietly, the astronomers enter the barn and give Mary gifts for the baby. One brings baby oil, one a soft warm blanket, and one a cuddly toy. Newspapermen and women soon arrive to hear the story. They telephone their newspapers. Soon the whole world knows about this special baby who was born in a barn.

Newsvendor brings on a new poster: 'A special baby has been born and his name is Jesus'. All children sing a carol.

Brenda Williams

Pull a cracker

Join the matching crackers and colour them the same.

Christmas tree

Put a star on top of the tree.
Draw presents underneath the tree.
Place decorations on the tree.

Piñata
Find and colour the sweets.

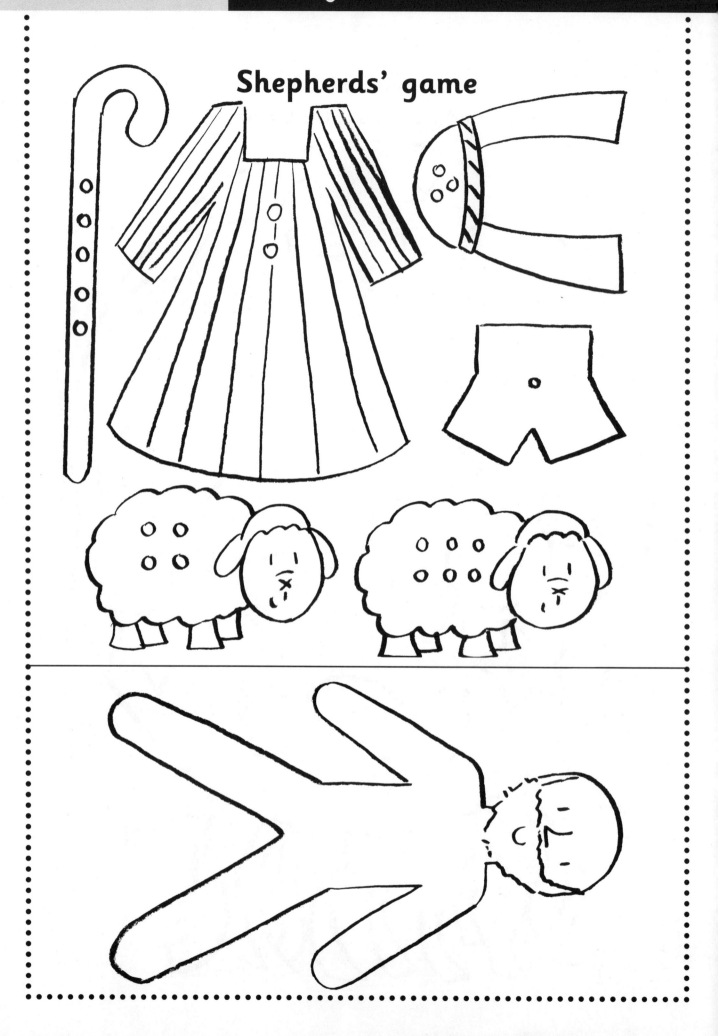

PHOTOCOPIABLE **Activity**

Letter to Santa

Father Christmas
Lapland

Dear _____

I hope you and your reindeer are well. My name is

_____, I am _____

years old and I live with _____

_____

in _____.

Could you please bring me

_____

_____

_____

_____

for Christmas. I have been very good.

Love from

_____

EARLY YEARS ACTIVITY CHEST *Christmas activities*

Christmas pudding truffles

To make the truffles

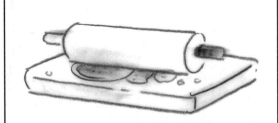

1 Crush two digestive biscuits on a pastry board using a rolling-pin.

2 Place the pieces in a small bowl.

3 Mix in the icing sugar and drinking chocolate powder.

4 Add the condensed milk and stir.

5 Roll the mixture into little balls in the chocolate strands.

6 Pour some icing on top and stick on holly leaves and berries.

7 Stick the truffles to some biscuits.

Christmas trees

PHOTOCOPIABLE Activity

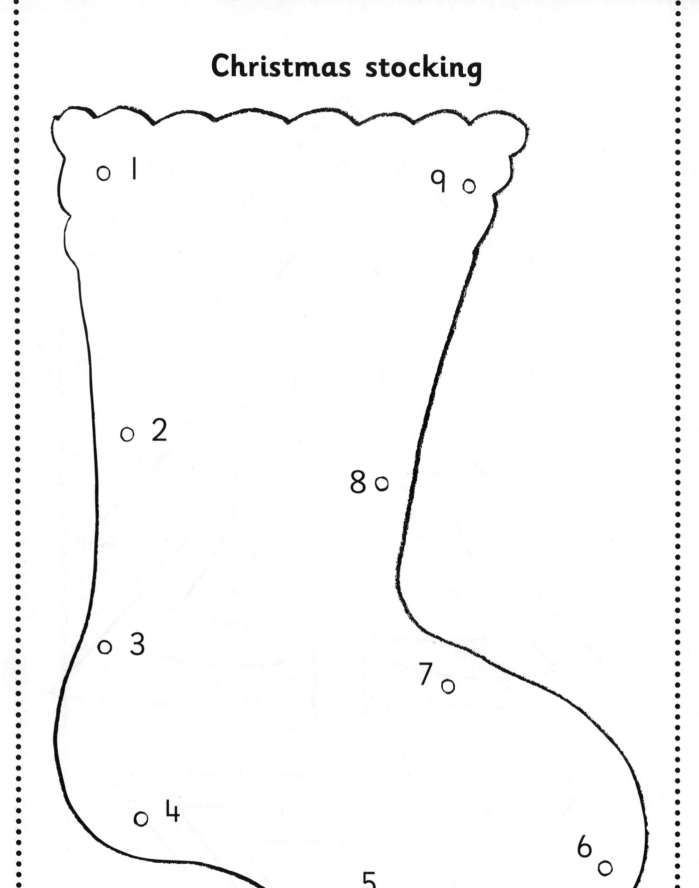

Christmas stocking

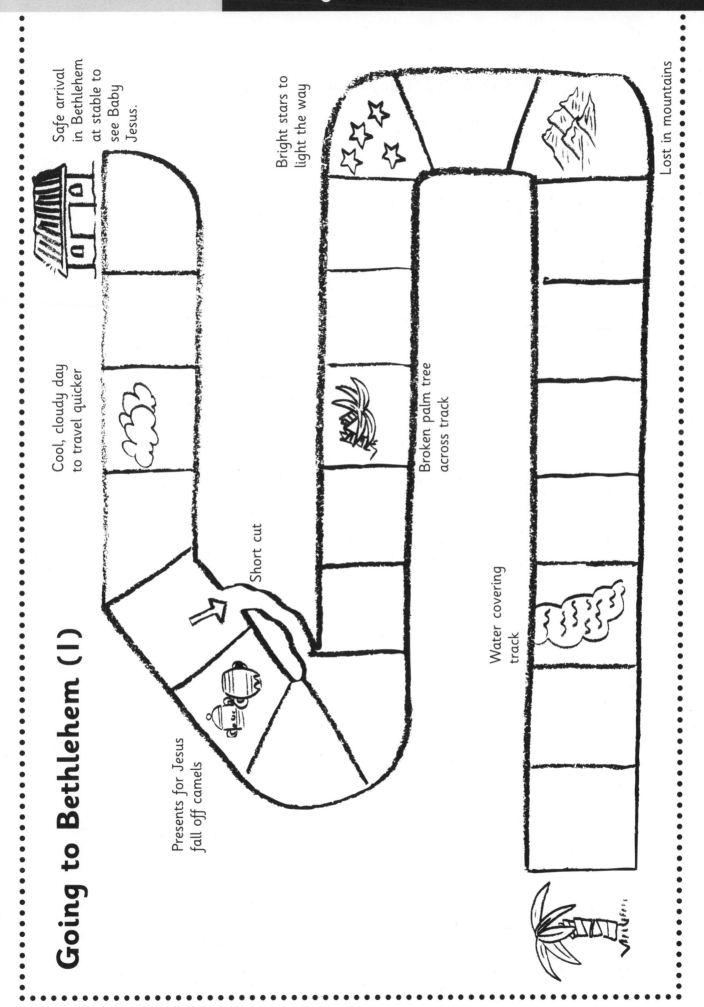

Going to Bethlehem (2)

 −1	 −2
 +2	 −1
 −1	 +1

Going to Bethlehem (2)

How many?

How many ☆ on the tree? How many 🎁 under the tree?

How many ⬤ on the tree? How many 🎀 on the tree?

How many 🍬 on the tree?

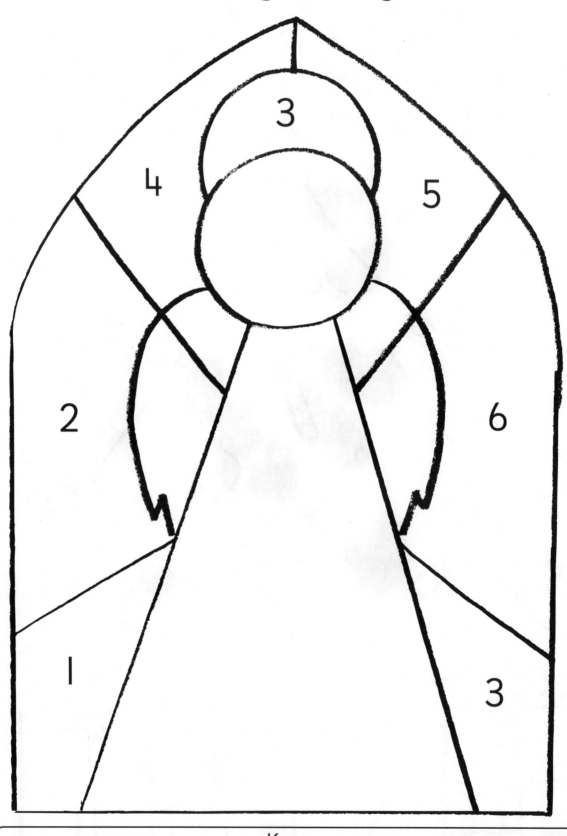

Play dough recipe

What you need

Ingredients
4 cupfuls flour
2 cupfuls salt
1 cupful water
4 tablespoons oil

Utensils
large mixing bowl
jug
measuring cup
wooden spoon
baking board
food colouring
white rice
brown powder paint
disposable gloves
airtight containers

To make dough
- Mix the flour and salt together in a large mixing bowl.
- Add the oil.
- Gradually add the water, stirring at first with a wooden spoon and then kneading with your hands.
- If the dough is too stiff, add more water.
- If the dough is too sticky, add more flour.

Varieties
- Separate out batches of dough and add different ingredients to make textured or coloured dough.
- Make a hole in the centre and add rice. Knead well to make a textured dough.
- Add a few drops of food colouring and, wearing the disposable gloves, mix well by hand.
- Add brown powder paint.

Coconut-ice balls

What you need

Ingredients
12 teaspoons coconut powder
9 teaspoons icing sugar
6 teaspoons condensed milk
pink food colouring
(This makes enough mixture for one child to make three coconut-ice balls.)

Utensils
small bowls
teaspoons
dropper
Cellophane
scissors
tray
pen
name cards
baking board
pieces of parcel ribbon

Method
- Use the dropper to mix a few drops of food colouring with the condensed milk.
- Add the coconut powder and icing sugar and mix well.
- Put the dough on a board, divide it up and roll into three balls.
- Arrange the balls on a tray and write each child's name on a piece of paper alongside their balls.
- Place the tray in the fridge to set.
- Once hard, invite each child to wrap their sweets in pieces of Cellophane, tied with parcel ribbon.

Action!

Sheep

Find the way

In a stable

Candy clay recipe

What you need
Ingredients
½ cup margarine
½ cup syrup
½ teaspoon salt
1 teaspoon vanilla, peppermint or strawberry essence
green and red food colouring
500g caster sugar

Utensils
teaspoon
pastry board
mixing bowl
measuring cup
wooden spoon
three airtight containers

Method
- Mix the margarine, syrup, salt, essence, food colouring (not for white batch) together to make a smooth paste.
- Add caster sugar, stirring with a wooden spoon and then kneading with your hands to make a smooth lump of clay.
- If the mixture is too stiff, add more syrup.
- If the mixture is too sticky, add more sugar.
- Transfer to a baking board and knead until smooth.
- Place the coloured candy clay in airtight containers.

Add
- vanilla essence to white candy
- peppermint essence to green candy
- strawberry essence to red candy